IN DANGER

A MEMOIR OF FAMILY AND HOPE

JOSEPHA DIETRICH

First published 2018 by University of Queensland Press
PO Box 6042, St Lucia, Queensland 4067 Australia

www.uqp.com.au
uqp@uqp.uq.edu.au

Cover design by Lisa White
Cover image by Nadia Masot, www.nadiamasot.com
Author photo by Amanda Hamilton
Typeset in Bembo Std 12/17 pt by Post Pre-press Group, Brisbane
Printed in Australia by McPherson's Printing Group

 **Queensland Government** This project is supported by the Queensland Government through Arts Queensland.

 Australian Government  **Australia Council for the Arts** The University of Queensland Press is assisted by the Australian Government through the Australia Council, its arts funding and advisory body.

ISBN
978 0 7022 5987 6 (pbk)
978 0 7022 6079 7 (ePDF)
978 0 7022 6080 3 (ePub)
978 0 7022 6081 0 (Kindle)

 NATIONAL LIBRARY OF AUSTRALIA A catalogue record for this book is available from the National Library of Australia

Josepha (Josie) Dietrich is an English immigrant to Australia. She lives in Brisbane in the home that she and her partner built on Passive House principles. After coming out of a long reign of being a carer, she's worked as a research assistant for universities on projects to improve psychiatric discharge planning and women's wellness after cancer. Her prior long-term work was in the After Hours Child Protection Unit, assessing children's risk of harm alongside the Sexual Offences and Child Abuse Unit of Victoria Police. To remain sane during this period, she flitted off overseas for months at a time to climb cliff faces while sleeping on beaches or in abandoned shepherds' huts. After her cancer treatments finished and in light of her experience caring for her dying mother, Josie joined the advisory committee of CanSpeak Queensland as a cancer and consumer advocate.

For my mother
Heather Mary Dietrich
21.02.1949 – 25.12.2005

Contents

Prologue

My mother's breast cancer was diagnosed when she was 45 and I was 21, an unwelcome third character in a story that, until then, had been ours. Just the two of us, friends and confidants, two moons circling each other. We shared everything.

From that day onwards my adult life was shadowed by the disease. It emerged every two to three years. Mum conceded to surgery but not to the chemicals. She sought solace in alternative therapies: Vitamin C infusions, a German non-chemical chemotherapy, psychic surgery and psychological work. They didn't save her.

But my mother's death saved me.

Four years after I buried her, my mother's cancer reared up in my own body. The minutiae of her experience – doctors' waiting rooms, hospital stays, waking up after a general anaesthetic with her breast off and a purple slash, the weighted realisation that her doctorate would never get submitted, the reckoning of a life – clawed deep into my own cells. Yes, I thought then, we did share everything.

Except for this: by then I had a child of my own, and I refused to share my mother's choices. Instead they galvanised me. I would fight for life with every piece of medical ammunition available. Chemical, surgical, atomic. In the end I had every female organ removed that could generate cancer, apart from my brain. I'm standing, still.

Diagnosis: will I live?

Cancer was named for the crab, because a cancer tumour sends claws out into the surrounding tissue.

Kathleen Jamie, 'Pathologies'

It was 6 p.m. on a Friday. I had Bolognese sauce boiling on the stove and the aroma of its red meatiness was in the air. The telephone burred.

When I answered, my GP didn't waste words. Josie, your results are in: you have ductal, invasive breast cancer. I've gone ahead and booked you in to see a breast surgeon on Monday.

I sat down at the kitchen table, my world now the size of its rectangle of silky oak. A tremor ran from my hand to my feet. A few days before, I had shaken uncontrollably as a doctor dug into my right breast with a fine needle, its journey guided by an ultrasound machine. I remember her authoritative voice warning me, This will sting. She pushed and the needle slid deeply into my breast. The sonographer, a well-kept woman in her early 50s, assisted. Something in that sonographer's manner and voice made me trust her immediately.

It turned out I needed both types of biopsies that day. The needle that poked in and out of the tumour to capture its adolescent cells, as well as a core biopsy, where a thicker needle shunted in and out to take tissue – like getting your ear pierced.

A support person, someone from the front desk or a training doctor, I never found out which, had stroked my hair back. She had a brown bob and a plump figure. You wouldn't notice her in a crowd unless you knew her and then you'd gladly rush over to share a confidence.

You're doing well, Josie, she'd said.

I wasn't. Not really. I'd wanted to say, I'm scared, I can't get a grip. My mind raced, looking for a way to escape what I knew then was coming.

Here you go, honey. She pressed a tissue into my hand.

I'd sobbed throughout the entire procedure, thinking of my mother, wave upon wave of memories lifting off my chest. Like me, she'd faced this painful procedure alone and later, like me, was alone when she heard the news. Did she think of her own death then, as I did now? The future and the present colliding, like the words of that faux Buddhist phrase on café walls: *Live like this is your last day on earth.*

That's what I read now in the aged, honeyed grain of the wood in front of me. I'd be dead in ten years, like my mother. And younger than she was, the flame of fate turned up high to reduce my lot.

I phoned my partner, B, at work and told him the results.

There was a pause and then he said, I'm on my way. He told me later he'd left his computer on with all his sustainable building projects unfinished. I pictured him like a missile on a radar screen, making his way closer and closer to our home.

While I waited I phoned my father without checking what time it was in England. When he answered I burst into tears. I don't want to die like Mum, I sobbed. My life is only half-baked. There's so much I want to do.

My father's faint Nottingham accent calmed me. I know, he said gently. I know, darling. But listen. Your mother's fate doesn't have to be yours.

I barely let him finish. But what if it is?

My father couldn't answer that question.

Celso stirred in his bedroom, pulling me out of myself. My nine-month-old boy had strawberry-blonde curls and a cherubic face, the high colouring only Caravaggio knew how to paint. I was still recovering from his traumatic birth, which we'd both only narrowly survived. His tiny body struggled, but he maintained a sunny sweetness. Would I live to see him grow? How would Celso, who so relied upon me to literally survive every day at this point in his short life, cope without the unconditional love of his mother? A similar question arose when my mother was dying. How would I cope without her unconditional mother love?

Celso's movements rustled the sheets around him. I went to him and plucked him from his cot, careful to avoid tugging on the tube that went up his nose. His skin still radiated the narcotic new-baby smell of fresh, warm straw. It's a powerful drug, designed to keep mothers bonded to their babies. I breathed him in and wondered if my mother might have made different decisions if I'd been an infant when she was diagnosed.

I placed Celso on his domed play mat and returned to the stove to stir the Bolognese. The window above the kitchen sink shone a rectangle of sharp light onto my hands.

B hadn't arrived home yet, but he was close. I saw myself as the large target on the screen with B about to connect.

When were you diagnosed? asked the paediatric surgeon.

Last Friday, I said.

Celso was on B's lap with the blood pressure cuff's black cord in his hand. He was tugging at it. I was taking off my faux-Burberry trench coat and feeling businesslike. *We're here to talk about my son's undescended-testicle operation, not my cancer.*

My lumpectomy's tomorrow, I continued.

His head reeled back. What's your treatment going to be?

I told him my plans. We got onto the subject of chemo-therapy baldness; he relayed the story of a colleague's wife who had alopecia and how people often mistook her for a cancer patient, so she wore a real-hair wig at home when guests arrived.

I think she looks great bald, he kindly added. So the operation's called orchidopexy. I'm basically moving the testis into the scrotum and sewing it in place. He looked at Celso: If all goes as planned I won't see you again until you're 16, buddy, and we have a man-to-man conversation about how to check your testicles.

B and I turned and smiled at one another. At this point in the reaving hell of it all, our son turning 16 was moon-landing material.

Before my diagnosis, I'd had a dream I would not forget. I was in a long room with iron-framed windows high up and neat rows of single beds, like a military hospital in the world wars. I looked at one bed, empty and firmly tucked in, a white sheet folded over a grey blanket. A line of writing looped along the seam: *Hospital Ward*. I looked around. In the other beds sick people lay and watched me. One of them asked me what I was doing.

I have breast cancer, I said, still staring at the sheet.

Lumpectomy: is this right?

Illness is the night-side of life, a more onerous citizenship.
Everyone who is born holds dual citizenship, in the
kingdom of the well and in the kingdom of the sick.
Although we all prefer to use only the good passport,
sooner or later each of us is obliged, at least for a spell, to
identify ourselves as citizens of that other place.

Susan Sontag, 'Illness as Metaphor'

Are you sitting down, honey? It was Mum's friend, Kath.

I am now, I said, half-laughing. I was 21 and living in a shared house in Brighton, Melbourne. I'd scored a cheap room in a once-handsome rundown brick bungalow with shag carpet and the largest bedrooms I'd ever seen. There were three of us in the house. We spent weekends rock climbing or catching up with friends in cafés on Brunswick Street.

Now I sat in the hallway of the house, with the Bakelite landline pressed to my right ear.

My mother came on the line. I don't want to tell you this. I'm sorry, darling, but I've got breast cancer.

Why? I asked, I mean how?

Patiently, my mother told me everything that had happened. It began, she said, when she noticed puckering under her left breast when she lifted it. I didn't want to scare you, so I went ahead and had the needle biopsy and mammogram to make sure I knew what was happening.

I remember the words formed images of hypodermic needles stabbing at my mother's chest. And her funeral.

How are you, Mum?

She'd started crying by this point. These last few years have been so bloody horrible I'm not surprised I've got cancer now, she said.

Mum had left her position as a lecturer in social ecology and the history and philosophy of science to live in the Northern Rivers and write up her PhD. The faculty she worked in had become too fraught with tension as her ex-partner's presence was a daily reminder of a bad break-up. Mum's PhD was on the development and innovation of genetically modified organisms in Australian society – how to devise public policy processes that avoided destructive conflicts and stalemates in decision-making. The move wasn't necessarily meant as permanent.

Several years after my mother's death I had contact with one of her last students, who said he remembered her as a charming, witty, super-intelligent woman with incredible compassion. There weren't many things you couldn't speak to Heather about, he said. Above all else, I remember her as a very strong woman who stood up for her beliefs, without ever denigrating anyone else's. She taught me that compassion and strength were qualities that should go hand in hand. In the three years I knew her, she made a huge contribution to my life and I believe she helped make me a better person.

My mother had been emotionally fragile all my life. It gave me, I think, a heightened sense of foreboding about losing her. My worst fear hovered in the shattered air around me as I sat on the floor in Melbourne, hundreds of miles away from her. As soon as I hung up I booked a flight north. I forgot about university lectures and assessment, about the rock I wanted to climb that weekend. It was the start of a pattern that would consume the next years: I would be regularly pulled by some internal magnet back to my mother's side.

I was a driven young woman studying statistical basics, brain functioning and varieties of theories behind why humans act as they do, according to Western psychology. Within the thick folders of background readings there were no how-to guides for a young woman to face adulthood without her mother.

I got on a plane and flew up to the Northern Rivers.

My mother's lumpectomy was performed at Lismore Hospital. As she lay in the recovery area after the surgery, I waited in her room. For some reason she'd been allocated a bed in the children's section, and the walls were plastered with colourful fairies. This cheered me – until a senior nurse came in. We need you to help with your mother, she said. She looked like someone trained on the wards before nursing went tertiary: no-fuss, capable. She's distraught, she said. We're worried she'll try to bolt. And she's disturbing the other patients.

I went in and Mum was open-mouthed hollering as if she'd woken from hell instead of a general anaesthetic. I leant forwards and held her face next to mine. I'm here, Mum, I said. It's over. The surgery's over. You're all right now.

Mum calmed down. I couldn't make my body move, she said. I woke in my head but couldn't get the nurse's attention.

Lismore is a town known for flooding, ferals, rednecks and a flourishing arts scene. I'd lived there for one year as a 19-year-old, studying philosophy of psychology and Japanese at the local university. I had my first adult relationship with a local GP, who was 15 years my senior and tried to help me calm my chattering mind with meditation. I kept the Vipassana practice longer than I kept the relationship.

In Melbourne, in my 20s, I found my people: climbers, thinkers, and eventually B. In the run-up I sought life with a capital L: travelling, sex, climbing, studying, drugs and dance, art. I was trained in feminism by a mother who'd fought since the 60s for equality. What was good for the gander was good for the goose. My body was mine to enjoy. I slept under a mosquito net in Thailand and climbed the country's limestone cliffs straight off white, sandy beaches; I taught climbing in Vancouver and sold outdoor kit to kind Canadians. I would tell them polypropylene thermals make you stink during long-haul trekking and to go for the merino ones instead. Sometimes women's cheeks would flush, though they were happy to have someone talk about it.

I returned from living in Canada early, after the news that Mum's original breast cancer had metastasised to the lining of her womb and surrounding organs. By this stage she'd married a very damaged Geordie. My mother was alone and unsupported in hospital because he didn't want to leave their dogs behind in the house. This was a precursor to what would come later. He wasn't looking after his wife, my mother, so I had to return to Australia to do so.

When Mum was first handed her ticket to the kingdom of the sick we had to cancel our real around-the-world trip. All the payments for tickets and hotel bookings in Tokyo, London, and Lake Victoria, Africa, were sent back to my mother's bank account to pay for her cancer treatment.

We never got to enjoy the thrills of travelling together on a mother–daughter adventure, though we did return to England together once to visit family, including my mother's adoptive and birth mothers – one of whom would be dead within four years of Mum's diagnosis of lobular invasive breast cancer.

I didn't know it at the time but my mother took a softly, softly approach to her breast cancer treatment. And as the dutiful daughter, I had to believe she'd make the best decisions to stay alive. She was an intelligent woman, a tertiary teacher. I assumed she'd know the right course to take. I didn't challenge her. In fact, I didn't know how to.

My own first cancer scare came in that same decade, when I was 28. It was taken seriously because of my mother's history, so an oncologist ordered a mammogram and ultrasound, and palpated me. She determined it wasn't cancer and didn't need a needle biopsy. I had pert, young breasts, but they were lump prone. I didn't believe I had cancer then, even though the process of meeting with an oncologist had frightened me. *My mother's story isn't going to be mine*, I'd said to myself.

Seven days after my GP's phone call, I walked into the Mater Private's surgical reception area. It resembled a European hotel. Some people were docked into booths with their iPods plugged in. Others held crisp daily newspapers fully opened and resting

along their own leg-table, ankle against a knee. The place had
the smell of a new car's interior.

But this freshly renovated waiting room was a false front.
Through the swing doors we would all endure the same naked-
ness, under cotton sheets with truckers'-sized see-through
knickers on. We wore constriction stockings to reduce the
risk of embolism from a slowed-down system under general
anaesthetic, and an unknown anaesthetist controlled our
breathing. Our lives in a stranger's hands.

The carpet was a close-cropped weave in a vibrant green
with darker squares. Its colour would come to represent how
I felt for months to come, its pattern nauseating.

My name was called and I went over to the middle-aged
nurse to go through my particulars one more time before
being admitted for surgery. She would check my weight
(53 kilograms), my height (163 centimetres) and my blood
pressure (86/60) before finally admitting me to the ice-cold
pre-op side behind the European foyer.

Do you know what procedure you're having today? she asked.

Oh yes, I knew.

My breast surgeon, Dr Wilkinson, a reserved man who
drove an old Valiant to work, would look down on my
unconscious body, take a scalpel from a nurse's hand and cut
into my right breast. He'd start near the cup of my waxed
armpit to perform the lumpectomy, to preserve the skin on
my breast.

He'd inject a kind of blue dye into my tumour and watch
it spread down the lymph tentacles to perform the modern
sentinel node biopsy. All the subterranean blue ones he would
cut out of my body. Part of my tumour would be sent to

America as I was a randomly assigned control subject in the BETH trial, which measured survival rates and the use of a drug, Avastin, on women with the HER2 gene.

For the next few years I'd get used to this. My cancer or, later, parts of my organs and tissues were outside me and in a dish. Packaged for transport and marked with information for an anonymous professional to slice into and analyse.

I often thought of all those pieces of me, the incisions and the excisions, bits passed to pathologists for testing or thrown into an industrial bin to burn to ashes that would puff out of the back end of a hospital. Although the only surgery where I would wake lighter due to the quantity of organ tissue removed was over the horizon – my double mastectomy. (Before meeting Dr Wilkinson I had already decided to have my breasts removed. It was the clearest decision to make – breasts develop cancer: get rid of them.)

My mother's bodily ashes I split – one portion under a gingko tree, the other lot into a stupa. Most of her is buried under the ancient species of maidenhair tree on my in-laws' former property. She grows on someone else's land now. The epitaph engraved on a brass plate in front of her contains the last two stanzas of Mary Oliver's 'In Blackwater Woods' poem:

> *Look, the trees*
> *are turning*
> *their own bodies*
> *into pillars*
>
> *of light,*
> *are giving off the rich*

fragrance of cinnamon
and fulfillment,

the long tapers
of cattails
are bursting and floating away over
the blue shoulders

of the ponds,
and every pond,
no matter what its
name is, is

nameless now.
Every year
everything
I have ever learned

in my lifetime
leads back to this: the fires
and the black river of loss
whose other side

is salvation,
whose meaning
none of us will ever know.
To live in this world

you must be able
to do three things:

to love what is mortal;
to hold it

against your bones knowing
your own life depends on it;
and, when the time comes to let it go,
to let it go.

Before burying the ashes under the gingko tree, I had gone to Chenrezig, a Buddhist institute north of Brisbane. That day I was all raw nerves. I had Mum's recently cremated ashes tucked under my arm like an infant; the mature bamboo creaking and clanking its trunks was another world death knell: death worked towards by the Buddhist practice of acceptance. I do not believe in renewal of a soul in the form of reincarnation, but the practice of calming your chattering mind and compassion and love – the hard-worked-for 'look to yourself; on the mat' type – has much value for me.

The smaller portion of her ashes was potted into a Tibetan shrine. She has settled there these past ten years among others in Chenrezig's sub-tropical gardens.

Three days after my surgery Dr Wilkinson phoned me with the news. The operation was successful. The margins were clear.

I repeated what he said, to clarify I understood it and to let B hear the results. We sat, hunched over, on the end of a single bed in our spare room. It was already afternoon and we hadn't bothered to open the curtain to let the light in. The door was closed and we could hear B's auntie on the other side entertaining our son in the lounge room. I didn't say much so

I could absorb what the surgeon was saying. I swallowed hard. His words came to me down the line as if by parachute – what was landing in my world?

But the surgeon was still talking: I removed nine lymph nodes from your armpit. One of them had a four-millimetre cancerous tumour. He paused. That's very small.

He told me when he held my lymph nodes in his hands they'd felt enlarged. This worried him, thinking all nine of them might be brimming with cancer cells flicked off from my breast tumour. I thought of the dried seaweed I'd picked up as a child from Sydney beaches. Dark green strings of discarded sargassum, which I imagined as mermaids' pearls. When I squeezed them between thumb and forefinger the pearls would give a satisfying pop.

Bugger, bugger, bugger, I thought.

B held my hand.

I asked the surgeon about the chances of the cancer spreading to the rest of my body. My voice was weak.

He spoke plainly, and I was grateful. I can't answer that, he said. Even your oncologist likely can't if there's no clear tumour. We'll do a CT abdominal scan and a full bone scan this week. With cancer tumours they can be in your lymph nodes, caught early and never rear up anywhere else, or it travels directly into your bloodstream, metastasises and kills you.

My head jerked away from the receiver. The words lit up in front of me: *I'm going to die. And before my son is ten.*

There's no escaping chemotherapy with these results, said my surgeon.

I didn't want to burst into sobbing tears, knowing that would quake B's insides, after all that we'd gone through as a couple already: our return from France for my mother's care then death, my near-fatal post-partum haemorrhage, and now the care of an as yet undiagnosed, high-needs baby.

When a child's spinning top turns, all the colours blend. At that moment I oscillated between *I'm going to beat this* and *My life's over* so rapidly that my emotions swirled into a fusion of optimism and dread.

They've caught it early though, right? B was churning through the information.

I nodded. Yep. But my internal voice added to my list of fears and regrets: *I'm fucked and I'm going to die without becoming an author.*

I had to put my ambitions on the back burner, again. When I had Celso, I put my Master of Arts in children and youth writing on hold. I finished the core subjects, a very rough draft of my novel and a decent draft of my exegesis, which examined how the hero's pathway, the journey towards knowledge and resolution, was best explored in young adult literature through dystopian narratives. My exegetical question was: *How has Ursula Le Guin altered the hero's pathway in her high fantasy* The Earthsea Quartet *(1968–1990), to fit changing contemporary social realities?*

Writing was now, again, the last thing I could afford to think about. Suddenly I was in the life-threatened category of people, of stories that only happened to others, to friends of friends or in magazine articles – not to *me*. I had grade 2 invasive ductal carcinoma and my cancer was triple positive: it had increased levels of oestrogen receptors, progesterone receptors and the HER2 protein (or human epidermal growth factor receptor 2 protein). Thanks to having been my mother's chaperone through her cancer days, I knew that after chemotherapy I'd go on hormonal therapy because of my cancer's oestrogen dominance. But just as suddenly I felt a spear of determination. I could do this. The job of chemotherapy and hormone therapy would be to cut off my cancer's food supply. It was not going to get me. I was going to starve it to death.

Body scans: what's inside me?

Look, let's look at you
crabbing disease that's taking over
my body
one nip at a time

I shook like I was standing on ice. The CT (computed tomography) scanner would laser-reach into my body, touch my soft tissue, stroke my rushing one-way valved blood vessels and bounce against my bones. The captured images from this internal sweep would show a medical expert, sitting in a distant room, if I had metastatic disease: *Ms Josepha Ruth Dietrich, CT scan for mets – invasive bc.*

I was screened off zoo-style from the medical staff, who stared in at me through a large glass pane. The walls of this private hospital room were beige and tired compared to the one where I'd had my lumpectomy one week before.

The bed in front of me was curved and slender, like a sleeping pod in some distant spaceship. I climbed aboard. The hospital gown protected nothing. I wore old, overstretched Bonds knickers and I didn't care.

Just stay still, said the CT scan technician standing by my side. Her manner was kind but businesslike. I could picture her playing volleyball.

A sting, then pressure, and a radioactive substance was injected into my vein via the inserted cannula. A metallic twang infused my mouth as though I were swallowing silver.

It'll feel like you're wetting your pants. You're not, don't worry, she said. She quickly turned and left the room, sealing the door shut.

It was the machine and me. It was spinning wildly 30 centimetres from my face. A disembodied male voice told me, Hold your breath. The machine whizzed around my torso then stopped: Breathe, said the same voice.

I hadn't stopped shaking from the moment I'd entered this room. I worried the CT image would blur. Warmth spread into my groin. I contracted my pelvic floor muscles just in case I *was* about to pee myself.

I'd consumed a litre and a half of some dodgy liquorice liquid and felt nauseated. A recurring theme throughout my treatment. The nausea and shaking had nothing to do with the liquid drunk or blood taken. I'd come out of the lumpectomy and sentinel node surgery one week earlier and the shock of being a 'cancer patient' was hitting home.

The CT slowed down. I hope they don't come out blurry, I said into the room, knowing the sonographer could hear me behind the glass viewer.

That's what I'm checking now, but all looks fine, said the sonographer through the two-way speaker.

Does that mean my internal organs look clear of metastases, when she said all looks fine? That's what I wanted to know.

All done! You can get changed now, she said.

I swung my legs off the bed and used a kindly pre-placed stool to get down.

Then I was sent back to sit in a yellow-walled waiting room. I recognised it immediately because I'd sat in a place like this as a 23-year-old while my mother had her CT scan. That day the MRI technician came out with a look I'd come to know well. Medical staff were invariably discombobulated when my mother collapsed with anxiety. She appeared to be calm and confident; she was articulate and looked directly into your eyes. People assumed she had it together.

And then the MRI technician and I were watching her emotional breakdown. My mother was sobbing, scared of what the doctors might find and the big medical machinery required to envelop her. Her physician needed a full bone and body scan. To get one my mother had to lie strapped down onto a thin bed as it moved into a hole in the wall. The technician looked unnerved; she flicked her gaze from my mother to me then to the machine. The concern could have come from not keeping to schedule, from the cognisance of a busy hospital day unfolding ahead of her.

I can't do it! They don't understand, my mother had said.

Her back was hunched over, her feet were planted firmly on the linoleum and she had a tissue over her open mouth. Her whole face seemed wet. I sat down with her and hugged her.

I'll hold your feet the whole time so you know I'm there, I said and made eye contact with the technician, who nodded approval then reached for the lead coat.

I would ground her, something I'd done my whole life. She was safe with me. And I was safe with her. I was loved unconditionally and knew it. I would never leave her like her own mother had at birth.

The MRI machine appeared claustrophobic; it was like watching my mother being posted into a crematorium kiln.

Patients cry in hospital because they're scared, because they've received bad news or simply because they're ill. I was reminded that day that my mother's crying wasn't like anyone else's. If the breadth of a mental health breakdown was a landscape, my mother sometimes appeared stuck in the middle of one, *Wuthering Heights* wild and on the verge of falling over a cliff.

As an eight-year-old I wrote a poem that said my mother's shoulders were made of fine-bone china. My teacher had me walk into the other classrooms with their low, metal-legged tables and read it aloud, as the other children stared up at me. I declared my mother's vulnerability to all my young peers in my *big* voice.

The world washed through my mother with its grief and joys. She told me she felt skinless most of her life.

In our Sydney days, Mum and I lived on the top floor of a three-levelled home, owned by an architect and a social work academic who specialised in critical reflective practice around dying, death and palliative care. Mum once flooded the bathroom so badly the water leaked down into the architect's study, destroying a project-in-process nicely displayed on his tilted drafting table.

Are you trying to become a fish and swim away, Piscean? I'd said to Mum on discovering her wildly throwing towel after towel down onto the bathroom floor to soak up the water.

She'd giggled, Yeah.

During the 80s Mum and our academic landlord and dear friend had a lot to do with women's rights around reproductive health. I went with Mum to a conference in Canberra, *Liberation or Loss?*, organised by the National Feminist Network on New Reproductive Technologies. I was 12 so I went into a well-run day-care-type setup on the Australian National University's campus. That many women in one place meant that many mothers needed their children minded so they could give lectures, run workshops (like my mother did) and attend talks.

During the writing of this book I approached our lovely one-time landlord (who became a family friend) for insights on my late mother's feminist and adoption activism during the 80s and early 90s. It was a period of time when I was too caught up in my own childhood and early adolescence to remember or know how my mother, as an adult, operated in these other worlds. Your mother harnessed the pain of her own experience to advocate for social change, she said.

I agreed, reflecting that I too leveraged my own experience, as my mother's carer then later as a breast cancer patient, to advocate for better health outcomes for those affected by cancer. A different agenda, but one equally imbued with a need to make a difference where possible. Mum was driven to change the laws around what she called *the black hole* of an adopted person's parentage because her own experience of this informed her very existence. She did not want women to experience shame and stigma, like her birth mother had, just for having a child out of the sanctioned environment of marriage to a man.

Heather, our friend continued, was a policy activist who championed for good social policies that didn't mirror the harm done by her own experiences, harm and distress that was ongoing. She acted against exploitation and commodification of women's bodies. Though she had the imagination to be able to reach across her principled position, like me with my son.

I'd babysat this friend's adopted son and taken him swimming in the pool next to Luna Park. He was a sweet, gentle soul whom I'd loved. As a budding photographer I'd taken his picture as part of my portfolio to get into Mr Kovak's class at the Canberra college I changed to in my last year of school. The focus was sharp and you could see the white squares of the window frames he sat next to reflected in his eyes.

I guess political and personal practice don't always speak together, our friend said. That's likely the case for you and I also.

Mum sat on the National Bioethics Consultative Committee (NBCC), formed in 1998 as an advisory committee to the Australian federal government. After the Liberation or Loss? conference the NSW Women's Advisory Council formed a working party to push for a national body to oversee the use of new reproductive technologies – hence NBCC. Mum represented a feminist perspective on emerging technologies that moved beyond the then-current concerns about artificial insemination by donor (AID) to issues like in vitro fertilisation, surrogacy, genetic engineering and euthanasia. AID now seems archaic as a concern at all.

NBCC disbanded the year we moved to Canberra: 1991. My mother and Sister Regis Dunne were the only two dissenters on NBCC's final report endorsing legalised surrogacy. NBCC was reformed into a committee with a more medical framework and stands today as the Australian Health Ethics Committee.

We went on to talk about her grandchild and my son. Our old friend's Scottish burr made me smile. After all these years in Australia her birthplace still counted in her vowels.

But now after my own CT scan to check for metastases I rattled off to the change room and got dressed. Then I returned to the waiting room for my full-body bone scan. I had the results of the first procedure in my hands, in a sealed envelope.

I went alone to these and other tests because Celso's level of care meant it was easier if he stayed at home with B, close to all the paraphernalia required to keep him going: compounded Losec in the fridge to control vomiting or at least reduce the scorching of his throat the vomit caused, spare nasogastric tubes in case he pulled one out, tape to secure the tube to his face, nappies, special formula bags …

You're skinny, said the assistant. The belt doesn't usually fit all the way over. She continued, I'm doing this so you can't move when the scanning commences, otherwise the bone scan won't work.

There was an easy-going rapport between the head technician and her student. Photographs of their families were Blu-Tacked to the walls. Both were from Malaysia.

I was one of many patients they'd scanned that day for various reasons: cancer, osteoporosis, et cetera. As I lay dead still and listened to their conversation, I wasn't Celso's mother, I was just another female patient with breast cancer.

I *was* slim. The only body change I'd noticed before my breast cancer diagnosis was significant weight loss. I put it down to returning to my pre-baby body, but enough people had commented to make me aware I was skinnier than normal. My smaller frame on the tiny bed made me feel almost childlike.

I lay there and felt relieved I wasn't being posted like a parcel, as my mother had been. Instead a large metal plate hovered within licking distance of my face to scan my skull and brain. It shifted further down, in shuddering jolts, to trace the contours of my body.

If I panicked I knew I could get out of the contraption by wiggling my arm out of one restraint and ripping the other off. I closed my eyes and tried to blank my mind.

What did it? I wondered. To get breast cancer ten years earlier than my mother. Maybe it was the oestrogen I'd taken to override my polycystic ovaries and their tendency to shut down the release of ripe eggs. Or could the hormones that flooded my blood during pregnancy have led to my cancer? Was it that pill that made my breasts lactate more? Would it have been less serious if I'd turned up to my regular breast check?

In the first seven weeks of Celso's life I'd fed him either a full bottle of breast milk or a combination of my milk and formula. My supply dropped easily so I kept up my continuous expressing with a white pill that made my breasts produce milk.

I'd hired the handbag-sized breast pump direct from the hospital chemist after Celso was born. Attached to it I'd felt like a milking cow with two udder teats instead of four. Its yellow, electronic arm swished back and forth to measure out suction strength and timing. The first few times I was amazed at the rush of warm, opaque milk into the plastic funnel and how the spray hit the bottom of the bottles with a thud. I'd known when the splat sound disappeared that I had expressed more than ten millilitres and was on my way.

In the morning my breasts had been like fists that needed coaxing to relax and open up, letting their contents fall out. When the tension eased the relief was satisfying, but not pleasurable. My mother had once confessed to me that breastfeeding was sometimes better than sex. The letdown of milk releases a hormone also released by physical affection and orgasm. Self-enjoyment aside, I'd missed the nuts-and-bolts action of being a mother and of breastfeeding skin to skin – to provide the best nourishment – for Celso.

When I had stared down with pride at my pregnant belly I'd conjured snapshot moments of my future when He or She and I were cocooned together on a couch or at an outdoor café enjoying the simple life. I couldn't wait to breastfeed, and show my baby off. When Celso refused my breasts immediately after birth and took the bottle, and even that reluctantly, a protective casing shucked off and I was raw and vulnerable.

I can't feed my baby! I'd said to the hospital nurses, thinking I was a failed first-time mother. They assured me it would come. It never did.

At home after Celso's birth we hired a clear crib on tall casters and wheeled him around the house so that we could see and hear him at all times. His floppy newborn neck allowed his head to drop to one side, where he'd commune with his reflection on the plastic walls. My Welsh uncle said that Celso looked like an angel. We were relieved it wasn't Angelman's, which the paediatrician flagged during my son's first post-hospital visits as a possibility. A Dr Angelman had a syndrome named after himself: these severely disabled children loved water like toddlers do, but unlike most toddlers they would never develop normally.

After Celso's birth, I almost didn't make it to the cancer diagnosis.

You might lose your uterus. We won't know until we open you up.

I was lying on a gurney with B behind me telling me he loved me and kissing my hair. I was in and out of consciousness, but when I was alert, I psyched myself up with *I have a child now. We could adopt the next time.* This played on repeat in my mind as I said to my stoic Irish obstetrician, That sounds a bit heavy.

Within five minutes I scrawled something like my name in red ink on the bottom of a medical 'do anything to save my life' consent form. Celso was in the neonatal intensive care unit, mainly because I was out of action and couldn't feed him, and B was potentially about to become a single father and needed to make medical decisions on my behalf. Celso had been born with a stridor, a loud breathing sound signalling something was wrong with his larynx, but scored normally on his Apgar test: seven then eight.

It's 2 a.m., why are all these people here? Exhaustion from a 25-hour labour, a caesarean and powerful painkillers had altered my state of mind. I sat on the operating table as a burly, pierced man clamped my head with two bear-like hands and my anaesthetist put in the second epidural. My body was gripped by the shakes. The obstetrician's sense of humour had returned now that the transfused blood was working and surgery was imminent. You look like a truck's hit you, she said.

It has, I replied, staring at the linoleum of the surgical theatre.

I woke up in the intensive care unit with an efficient nurse flapping around me. Mechanised tights, the medical version of leg warmers, pulsed up and down my calves to prevent deep vein thrombosis. The brown-eyed nurse picked up an intimate conversation with me as soon as she saw me stir, as if my waking had merely interrupted what we'd been saying, like we were two old friends. The possibility of dying in childbirth sends a shudder of horror through any woman, including nurses. I'd lost over four litres of blood from a massive post-partum haemorrhage. From kind strangers I had received 13 units of A+ blood. The relief of surviving the intensity of the situation, and of knowing my son was okay, relaxed me for the first time in a very long day.

The walk to the shower involved a rolling stand holding all my intravenous lines for medications, a nurse, and one of those frames the elderly use to walk to the shops. I was the medical version of an octopus.

An on-call obstetrician had saved my uterus. I remember seeing him slapping his own face to heighten his alertness – he'd arrived straight from his bed at home. When he walked up to my ICU bed I shook his hand. Thank you for saving my life, I said.

No worries, he replied. Next time, have a planned caesarean.

The irony was that if I'd lost my uterus after my son's birth it would've been one less thing to contemplate removing a year on.

Until Celso's surgery for a juvenile larynx at four months, his breathing was laboured and noisy. After surgery he couldn't take bottled milk (he had still never managed to breastfeed) or keep any food down – at all. Little did I know at the time that watching Celso drinking from those initially heartbreaking bottles would be something I'd come to crave. Soon he would need a feeding tube. Life with my son was harried and the days were long, but they also passed as quickly as the crack of a whip. There was no time for anything else. Not even my regular breast checks.

Being a carer, where you're forced to put another person's life ahead of your own, fitted like an itchy, tight woollen jumper. I went to pull it over my head and it stuck across my shoulders. I couldn't get it off, so I smoothed it back down over my chest. Celso played happily at my feet, but my head often lifted up to the horizon where I mentally planned my escape back into my brain. I thought this forward planning a sign that the mountainous road we'd been walking on as a family was levelling out.

Then the cancer diagnosis arrived.

After both the scans I stood on the street and simply breathed for a while. The entrance to the old veterans' hospital was off a laneway; nearby a metal sword was thrust vertically into stone to mark the grave of the slain warrior, and of Christ. In front of me a courier dropped off a document and jogged back to his car. The world continued to spin in its normal way, but my world had shrunk to two envelopes. My future was in my hands, but I was in no rush to see it. Standing there, I felt the temporary relief of not knowing. Unopened, the results were a choose-your-own-adventure novel: one way led to surviving, the other …

It was peak hour so I phoned B. I'll catch a bus into the city then get home on the busway, I said.

On the way I went into Myer and bought myself a red handbag with zebra-print lining. Buying it cheered me up, but a buzzing in my stomach akin to nerves told me I had to get home to see Celso. The emotional cord that stretched between him and me pulled my attention back if I spent too long away, as it had when I cared for my mother.

On the bus I opened my scan results and read the doctor's notes. There was, they said, no evidence of metastatic disease.

Portacath: could I think my way out of cancer?

Despite technological advances, the most useful tool available to a doctor remains their patient's voice.

Gabriel Weston, *Direct Red*

Welcome! my interventional radiologist boomed into the waiting area. He stood looking down at me on the trolley. He was mid-40s, with well-combed short hair and a likeness to many men I'd danced with platonically in the 80s as an underage raver in Sydney. He was going to fit a portacath into my chest by inserting a ten-cent-sized pincushion under my skin above my left breast; sewn in place the portacath's tail would thread up and over my left clavicle and into my jugular vein. Chemotherapy would deliver its chemical power straight into my heart.

I piped up at him, There's a letter from the anaesthetist who did my lumpectomy about drugs to avoid. I get intensely nauseated.

I've read it. Don't worry, because I'm sending you into a twilight zone. You're not going under a GA. Most people don't wake with nausea. You're actually conscious and able to speak with me; you just won't remember anything you've said.

But I want to know what I've said.

Yes, I've had some interesting conversations. He stared up into the room's cornice with a faint smile on his face as if recalling some former patient's obscenities.

What if I say odd and embarrassing things?

He shrugged and smiled. See you soon.

I returned to reading *The Brain That Changes Itself* on brain plasticity. It was the chapter on pain where Norman Doidge told the story of the neurologist Dr Ramachandran, a renaissance man who'd assisted an amputee patient, Philip Martinez, to successfully 'amputate' a phantom limb by fooling the patient's brain to 'see' his amputated hand move using a mirror box. The intense pain of Philip's frozen elbow disappeared after one month.

Medical memoirs and readable medical books interested me in general, but my growing fears about Celso's development made me seek out stories of atypical learners, stories about people whose behaviour or brain functioning made them appear 'retarded', a 'playful' insult unfortunately still bandied around today. It pulls me up every time I hear it. I wanted the stories of those who, in adulthood, finally functioned well in communicating their intellect or thoughts with others. They could still be atypical, just independent. (My searching would eventually lead to a play-based therapy, the Son-Rise Program, that did indeed begin to 'awaken' my son.)

Five trolleys were lined up side by side with no screens. I was on the far right. Covered in white blankets, and looking down the row of men and women dressed in white theatre gowns, I glimpsed a shimmering aura of emotion, almost physical in its presence. A young man held his body stiffly. He grimaced when he moved and stared straight up into the ceiling. The woman next to me had a round face. She was wearing a loosely knitted beanie and peered about with curiosity, as if she was at a party and hadn't been introduced to anyone yet. I avoided eye contact so I could read.

What are you here for? she said by way of introduction.

I'm getting a portacath put in, I said, and returned to my reading.

I came here to get mine out.

I put my book down. What did you have it for?

Breast cancer.

Who's your oncologist?

She had the same one as me, and said that she thought the oncologist was lovely and always dressed well.

I agreed with her about the dressing-nice bit.

She told me about the alleged side effects of one of her chemotherapy drugs, Taxotere, but she'd experienced none of them apart from tiredness.

You're lucky, I said. I hope I have the same run as you.

Yeah, she said. She was likely somebody's grandmother; I could see her sharing a sponge cake with a child and pouring pretend tea into plastic cups for as long as the child wanted to play the game. This woman had travelled lightly through breast cancer treatments. I envied her.

My sprightly radiologist swung back into view. He and a surgical nurse wheeled me down a short corridor towards the operating theatre. I checked the doctor's name on my identification wristband.

I pointed to my left wrist. There's a different doctor's name on my tag here.

Yes, Dr _____. He's operating in the other theatre. There have been some changes to the roster of patients. You can have him if you like.

No, I like you. And I did. My interventional radiologist was kind.

Good, I like you too. His nurse wheeled me in. The atmosphere in the room was of professionals who had worked many graveyard shifts and had established a playful manner with one another. My name replaced the previous patient's – another woman – on the computer display screen, which hovered above the table.

Someone's been knitting in here, said a young nurse. He untangled a black, rubber slinky with a probe on the end that clipped onto a person's toe or finger to measure the oxygen levels in their blood.

I was shaking. My nerves were swamped – again – like they'd been the day I had my CT scan.

The anaesthetist who sedated me for my lumpectomy wrote a letter suggesting TIV (total intravenous anaesthesia) to reduce post-operative nausea. For days after the lumpectomy I'd experienced waves of intense *I'm going to vomit* surges, that hospital's green carpet rearing up at me again and again. Being on my back, about to be put under and operated on so soon after my lumpectomy, even for a minor operation, made me fearful. The shaking went all the way inside to my mind. If there were grab bars above my bed I would've clung to them, trying to centre myself, knuckles white. *Give me some control.*

Later on another anaesthetist, a female one, got the cocktail right and informed me that the days of nausea after my lumpectomy were likely due to a reaction to the anti-emetics, not the anaesthetics.

The portacath procedure was straightforward. I didn't get sick this time, and once the drugs were out of my system I could leave. I phoned B to come and collect me from the front so he didn't have to get Celso out of his baby seat.

After I healed I headed to the Royal Brisbane and Women's Hospital (RBWH) to get an echocardiogram: an ultrasound scan of the heart. I was the youngest by 15 years or so in the waiting room – this had invariably been the case since my diagnosis.

The 'echo' checked my heart function and provided a base reading before chemotherapy's rotgut commenced. My chemo regimen was TCH (Taxotere, Carboplatin, Herceptin). On Herceptin's list of common side effects, first off the rank was moderate to severe heart failure. The uncommon side effects were acute respiratory distress syndrome (acute onset of severe shortness of breath) and pulmonary fibrosis (chronic lung damage).

My oncologist needed to know if there were changes to my heart after TCH started, so I would have an echo performed every ten weeks. They took about 15 minutes, but today's took three-and-a-half hours; the sonographer had to rush to a patient who had arrived in accident and emergency. No worries, I said. I was inside a large, quiet room. The lights were low and before she left the sonographer grabbed a blanket to throw over me; she bustled out of the room swinging her ample hips. I had the whole place to myself. No one could contact me. I went into a heavy sleep and woke later to my sonographer apologising for the delay. Then she squirted some warm gel onto my chest before wielding the ultrasound probe to see if this tin woman had a heart.

Chemotherapy: are genes us?

I felt my life with both my hands
To see if it was there —
I held my spirit to the Glass,
To prove it possibler —

I turned my Being round and round
And paused at every pound
To ask the Owner's name —
For doubt, that I should know the Sound

Emily Dickinson

I was in the day oncology unit at the RBWH in Herston. It had taken some juggling for B to get some time off work, and for us to organise carers to travel from interstate to look after Celso. My mobile rang. Celso doesn't need to be admitted, so we're heading home now to put him to bed. Call me before you finish today, said B. Relief flooded through me, but the memory of Celso's phlegmy chest sucking for air on our sofa at home and his sweaty face from a high temperature stayed in my mind. The danger to his small, lethargic body trumped everything on this day – my first chemotherapy day.

Our son's godparents, partners Ngaire and Mieke, were in Brisbane to assist us as a family through that first chemotherapy session, and responsibility for the two patients was split between B and our friends. B with Ngaire had prepared for the possible admission of Celso and all that entailed: overnight bag, toys, medication, vomit rags, books, his favourite owl with a bell in its belly that jangled when he shook it. B then sat in the Royal Children's Hospital accident and emergency department, ten minutes' walk away from the oncology unit, with Celso and a GP note.

Mieke was with me, likely girding her loins against the emotion of walking into the hub of cancer care, with all its reminders of life's frailty. So used by then to repeat visits to accident and emergency with Celso, B and I clicked into automatons. B phoning with the news that there wasn't another admission decelerated the carer-train thoughts of *What next, what next, what next?* Despite those sticky memories of Celso's distress, I could focus on what lay ahead.

The hospital and medical research complex in Herston was so vast it had its own postal code. B's engineering company had one report that estimated the air-conditioning units there alone used enough energy to fan 30,000 homes.

The walk to the RBWH took 15 minutes. We'd crossed the road from my house and walked up the steep street; either side was lined with Australian ivory curl trees, their young leaves split and splayed like storks' feet. On my left were two houses dedicated to the families of children going through intensive cancer treatments. Often a parent stood outside smoking and staring at the ground. I turned right and away from these houses and walked up a steeper road to the back entrance of the hospital complex. This was the business end, with delivery docks and energy towers piping out mist. One dock near my turn-off to the day unit had the ominous title 'neonatal collection'; the doors were always shut and smoke billowed out of a furnace. I saw the smoke as ashes of dead babies, even when I tried not to.

While we waited inside, my concern for my son's health still took my mind off my own. I kept my mobile in my hand in case B phoned with a scary change.

Will you wear a wig? Mieke and I chatted about whatever came into our minds as we sat on the crammed waiting-room chairs. After decades of making Australia her naturalised home, she maintained a Dutch stress on words and said *I sink* instead of *I think* – a charming pronunciation.

I nodded. I'll buy one before I go bald.

I think it'll suit you. Mieke smiled with her entire face, her bright blue eyes twinkly.

A chubby nurse with badges on her shirt called us both down the hall to the oncology rooms. The chemotherapy preparation room had a DVD player, pamphlets on every subject to do with cancer and its treatments, and two floral print couches.

Everyone starting chemo watches this video, she said.

Okay! I got across to the nurse that I didn't want to talk any further, so she left Mieke and me alone.

I turned to Mieke. I'll be fine in here. Would you mind going home to help B?

Are you sure? Ngaire's with B. Mieke held my gaze and saw that I really was okay with her leaving. She hugged me and I closed the door behind her. In fact I *wanted* to be alone. Inside I was about to crack.

It was my habit to retreat inside myself at times of intense stress or emotion, and I preferred to do it without an audience. It was as if I needed to shut the noise off – of conversations or communicating with someone else – to inhabit my inner world. I looked up at the ceiling to try and stop tears falling out of my eyes. I planted my hands on my hips while I slowly paced around the room, thinking, *I'll survive this, I'll survive this.* Out of the corner of my eye, I watched the video about other people's stories of chemotherapy and how they'd coped with it. The footage of patients reflecting on their cancer treatment was a way of stepping through a door from one reality into another.

Before this first day, I'd searched hungrily through *The Emperor of All Maladies: A Biography of Cancer* for Barbara Bradfield's name. Dr Siddhartha Mukherjee told the story of how a fast-tracked trial of the drug Trastuzumab (Herceptin) saved her life, then later many lives when it came onto the market in the 1990s. It was about to save mine.

After Barbara's first lot of unsuccessful treatments, her pregnant daughter was killed in a car accident. Then her aggressive cancer flared up again. However, after receiving Trastuzumab, she survived the tolling bells of 'terminal' cancer and extraordinary grief. She remains alive today.

Cancer genes come from within us; the unique chromosomal make-up in our cells was written with the potential to develop cancer. We're *loaded* with cancer genes – oncogenes – but they need to be activated for cancer to develop, for instance by an infection or a mutation in another gene.

When I was diagnosed my family paid for the BRCA1/ BRCA2 genetic test to see if I'd inherited either of the known breast cancer genes. I received the result within a fortnight and it was negative. The truth was that even though my mother was diagnosed with breast cancer at 45 and I was diagnosed at 35, no one knew why. I stood in the room with two pieces of good news: I didn't have a known faulty gene and the cancer was gone from my breast and armpit, which bolstered me against my fears.

But the procedures required to test for mutant genes or remove flesh that held the result of bad genes were nothing in the face of what I was about to experience. I was taken out of the introductory room to a windowless space where nurses accessed portacaths and took bloods. It was as if I'd walked around the butcher's counter to the super bright, cold refrigerator out back. I expected the room to go black and icy when a nurse closed the door. I would come to learn that nurses never closed that door because of feelings of claustrophobia.

Take a deep breath, said the nurse. I later befriended her when she became my regular nurse. She told me a difficult story of her first baby, who had died soon after birth, and how she'd come to call Australia home. She'd moved countries to escape her mother tongue: it embodied the memory of her lost child. She held the puncture kit of round, white plastic with its metal proboscis and IV line attached over my recently inserted portacath.

One, two and three. She pushed it through the septum of the port beneath my skin. Plunk.

No pain. I didn't feel it. Thank you.

Good. She smiled and winked.

I smiled back.

Over several hours I was plugged and unplugged into my chemo cocktail. My face went hot, and then I went cold. My heart beat faster for a while, but I was also nervous.

Brenda Walker's *Reading by Moonlight* explored how books saved her while she went through treatments for breast cancer. She realised her third novel, *Poe's Cat*, was an echo chamber of the ideas she'd worked on throughout her writing life, and that the writers so familiar to her, such as Edgar Allan Poe and Samuel Beckett, wrote similarly about their emotions not wholly stabilising after terrible experiences. I wondered if this was going to be my story too. I took a sip of tea and ignored my own enquiry. It wasn't too bad.

At first.

Mieke and Ngaire had to return to Canberra in the afternoon, so I opted to walk home after chemotherapy, as B couldn't bring our sick son into the oncology ward. I looked over at the parents smoking outside the childhood cancer houses with greater empathy this time.

Happy birthday to you, happy birthday to you, happy birthday dear Celso, happy birthday to you.

It was the fourth of July and our son was surrounded for his first birthday party by his family: his paternal grand-mother, who had jumped out of retirement into heading an International Baccalaureate college; his maternal grandfather (my dad) and aunt (my youngest half-sister), both arrived from the south of England; his great-aunt and great-uncle from B's side, who lived in Brisbane; and three of Celso's first cousins once removed. I helped him blow out the candle.

I cut the Mediterranean orange cake I'd made that day. It was for the adults as my son didn't eat, but it was still incredibly important to me that I bake his first birthday cake. I'd commenced chemotherapy the week before and didn't want to fail as his mother on the day he turned one in the world.

My brain was strung out and my stomach was raked by hunger; the chemotherapy had begun its stripping-down effect, where your higher thoughts and feelings turn basic. At the time of Celso's birthday I still had the mental capacity to think about what might come if I didn't survive. However, over the horizon was a time where simple survival instincts were all I had left – I could hardly factor him into my daily cancer routine, let alone parent effectively again.

I bit into the cake. Oh, not good! Does it taste bland to you or is it my chemo mouth?

Everyone politely said that it was a little savoury but okay.

It was tasteless. I realised I'd put in too little sugar – or none at all.

The following morning I couldn't get warm.

Are you all right? My father was in and out of the spare-room-slash-study getting me a breakfast of porridge with prunes, and a cup of tea.

No, I don't feel great actually. Could you get another duvet? I'm cold. I huddled under the pile of bedding, trying to sleep.

B had gone to work and my father was minding Celso. In between I supervised his nasogastric feeds.

My father and my sister Alex were staying in a nearby hotel because our house was too small for multiple guests. It was a two-bedroom post–World War II Queenslander with ornate ceilings and solid glass-panelled doors, the size of an apartment but on a proper-sized house block.

When Alex arrived at our home near midday and took to reading a *Spot* book to Celso, I had flushed cheeks and my throat was raw. I took my temperature and drew a reading of 39. I better go to A & E, I told my father.

If you're an oncology patient having chemotherapy, you get an emergency card. You flash it at the triage nurse to be admitted without waiting, as fevers and chemo are a bad combination.

My father and I were ushered into the emergency room. An experienced nurse walked up to us, held my father's hand and exchanged some English–Australian banter about England winning the Ashes, then pointed to a seated area near the green cubicles. She simultaneously showed authority and calmed my father and me down. If Mum hadn't briefly married an Australian man, *Green Card* style, we might never have stayed here. The reality of this sliding-doors moment came back to me; my father might have looked after me in situ instead of having to travel half a world to reach me.

I was ushered into a curtained cubicle and my history was recorded by an experienced though young nurse with streaky dyed-blonde hair. An elderly woman was outside in the white corridor on a trolley, with a male nurse asking her questions: Do you know where you are? Who do you live with? She was disoriented and couldn't answer him.

I lay back on the trolley and stared up at the fluorescent-lit ceiling. My father was allowed to enter and pushed the drapes aside like he was swatting a fly. He sat in the one corner without heart monitors or the mobile observations trolley with its blood pressure cuff, oxygen saturation probes and long proboscis thermometer.

Are your eyes normally this puffy? the nurse asked me.

No. I'm also not normally this flushed.

The nurse nodded. We'll get something for your fever once we know what's going on.

She wore one of the old-fashioned nurse's watches with only the face pinned to the left breast pocket so you could glance down to read the time.

I might have picked up my mother-in-law's cold. She arrived a few days ago, I said.

You're not supposed to see people with any infection once you've commenced chemotherapy, she said in a telling-off manner.

I didn't know at the time. *Fuck's sake, Josie. You were too blasé about contact with people.* I wanted to reverse time and pay more attention to that chemo introductory room.

Where did she arrive from? asked the nurse as she scribbled comments in my medical chart.

Hong Kong.

The nurse's head jerked up. Does she normally live in Hong Kong?

Yes.

My father's back straightened on the chair.

The nurse asked a lot of questions about my mother-in-law's presentation and whether she'd been tested for swine flu. No, she hadn't been tested, but, despite it being considered an epidemic at the time, I figured the chances of her having swine flu were remote as she was in charge of a school where health standards were high. The nurse went off to inform the doctor and get a quarantine card to attach to the now-closed curtain over my cubicle. Anyone who entered had to wear a mask and gloves. It wasn't quite code red, but definitely code pink, and after a throat swab that made me gag, and getting my nose poked, I was regarded as having swine flu until proven otherwise.

My doctor arrived, a newly minted registrar of oncology, and shepherded me through the situation and medical requirements. He was one of those rare men who matched a keen intelligence with kindness – eyes that reflected inwards as well as looking out – and he also had the endearing quality of speaking aloud his thoughts. He questioned me about my breast cancer in relation to my mother. I guessed where this was going, so said:

I'm not BRCA1 or 2 positive. There's likely an inherited unspecified cluster that's made me susceptible to breast cancer.

Oh, highly intelligent.

Alas no – just regurgitating what a highly intelligent geneticist with a name like Dr Gattaca said.

I did well in biology at school because I had a good memory for rote-learning details and finding sequences that linked information together in pictures. After studying I'd close my eyes and read off the image in my mind to answer test questions. This ability would evaporate after chemotherapy and induced menopause.

My fever remained constant at 38.5, and with no known source of infection the registrar had to get my blood tested. My white cell reading came back as 0.00. When a bacterial infection has no white cell soldiers to attack it, it attacks the organs directly. The registrar placed me on continuous antibiotics straight away, even though the full blood cultures were still not back from pathology.

I'm treating this as serious; you'll need to be admitted onto the oncology ward and likely stay up to five days, he said.

I searched for my father's eyes. They were fixed on mine. We couldn't believe it. The day before I'd attended my son's birthday party relatively well, and now I was febrile, with no white cells and possibly an unknown bacterial infection attacking my organs.

After a few hours in the accident and emergency cubicle I was wheeled up to the oncology ward and into a large isolation room because of the swine flu possibility. The oncology ward had rooms that ran off a central, carpeted corridor. There were only four single rooms as the rest had multiple beds of four or two in a room. I later found out the single rooms were for people *leaving us*.

I climbed onto my trolley-bed and looked through the open blinds out to a courtyard where a couple of medicos were smoking. A nurse wheeled a machine in to take my blood pressure and pulse. Its rubber wheels squeaked on the linoleum flooring. I looked up from my bed to the TV on its high mount. You had to pay extra to operate it, which I thought fair. The public system is burdened already, without footing patients' pay-TV habits.

After the nurse took my observations I grabbed the IV pole delivering my antibiotics and wheeled straight ahead into an industrial en suite with easy spray-down walls. I wanted to see all the corners of my isolation room.

The nurse assigned to me for that night came in and

introduced herself, and handed me a mask. Anyone who enters will be gowned up, she said, pointing to her own yellow smock, mask and blue rubber gloves.

People's eyes were all I would see for three days. I was a princess in my keep. Until day four when my cultures returned, proving I did not have swine flu.

A friend working as an investment banker in Paris sent me an email. *Contracting swine flu would've been just greedy*, he wrote. His and my friendship was cemented trekking in the Rockies together when we were 26. He had befriended my mother first on a self-analysis course he attended after a very painful divorce. Mum had said, He walked into the meeting room and had the same energy as you. I thought you'd make great friends. And we did.

I need to be travelling with someone like that, he'd apparently said after seeing a climbing photograph of me in the back of a Mountain Designs catalogue. Our friendship had started in email letters before we met in London for the first time.

Even though I had a casual boyfriend then, I secretly held out hope that this email friend might be the 'one'. That didn't turn out, but this dear, soulful banker taught me what decency in a man looked like. It was a quality I would later find in B.

After many blood tests the speak-aloud oncologist came in with the results. Your bacterial infection is treatable. These types of infections can be life-threatening for immune-compromised people like you. He was holding the results sheet with both hands.

Thank you, universe, I thought, and uncrossed my fingers. What did I have then?

The primary source of infection was bacterial, streptococcus from your stripped throat.

I put my hand up to my throat and swallowed: my oesophagus was a ribbed walnut.

The viral infection was a cold – a secondary concern for us really.

Okay.

Because I wasn't infectious I moved into a two-bed medical suite with an elderly man who had some type of severe rash and made strange rubbing sounds at night. In the morning a nurse with a short, straight-cut fringe came into my new room. You're young for breast cancer, she said after enquiring why I was there.

I know. I am. I was the youngest on the ward.

As my white cell count was too low I was classed as 'neutropenic'. My oncologist, who was in the early stages of pregnancy at the time, arranged for me to receive a G-CSF injection for free. G-CSF or granulocyte-colony stimulating factor is a haematopoietic (to make blood) growth factor. For people who become neutropenic, the Pharmaceutical Benefits Scheme provides a G-CSF injection. This medicine slow-releases over three weeks to stimulate the bone marrow to produce white cells to cope with the onslaught of chemotherapy. In three days my 0.00 neutrophil status was boosted to 23. Result. My white cell soldiers had returned: so too a functioning immune system. This was my first brush with the danger caused by the treatments to cure me and not by the cancer itself.

In my hospital isolation I managed to read one book: a complex novel by psychoanalyst Salley Vickers about human frailty, *The Other Side of You*, which matched the heaviness in my chest. I felt as if my heart had sunk. You'd think when faced with such ill health from a bad chemotherapy reaction you'd want only light comedy, but I didn't. I read works that helped me to access a language to describe my life.

The psychiatrist in the story had been traumatised by witnessing his brother's death as a boy. Vickers explores survivor guilt, something that was playing at the edges of my consciousness about my mother and not helping her make better choices.

Have you dusted off the TV yet? I asked B over the phone. It was time for the Tour de France, which we watched, religiously, every year. It was the only time we brought in the television from our house's understorey.

The first time we saw the Tour together we were lined up alongside many French people in Besançon, near the border with Switzerland, to watch the time trials. We'd driven south like mad things from our then home, a shared apartment in Strasbourg, camping overnight on the wet undergrowth of a forest close to the highway. Preceding the cyclists was a procession of floats. Our favourite was a huge, pink pig that rumbled by with a man throwing lollies. Hot croissants and black coffee were on hand, served out of stainless steel trolleys.

I looked away from my own TV and held the hospital phone close to my ear. Can you come in and see me? I asked.

B paused. I can't, pea. I'm in lock-down mode. I don't want to bring any infection into your hospital room – can't risk a repeat of what just happened. Your father's visiting you, isn't he?

I wanted to see B, but said, Yes, Dad was here today. We talked about my grandfather and his World War II service.

My grandfather oversaw the making of second-rate tanks, in Nottingham, for the British government, who were sending their troops over to fight the Germans in their superior tanks.

How's Celso going? I asked.

He seems fine with my mum. He's likely missing you but getting a lot of attention, so nothing to worry about.

Are you doing the feeds?

Yeah, it's all sorted.

How is he going down to sleep?

Mum's got him in bed with her, which he prefers.

Tell him I love him. Let's put me on speaker next time so I can talk to him. How are you?

Pause. Good, B replied.

All right, I said. The Tour's starting, are you watching it?

Yep, about to have dinner, love you.

Love you, good night.

The Tour is a physical and psychological minefield of pain and intense joy for the participants; it's about perseverance, which was what drew me in every year. American Lance Armstrong was famous for winning the Tour de France seven times, and then having the medals taken away. He also made a miraculous return to professional cycling after advanced testicular cancer. Lance's cancer story in *It's Not About the Bike* inspired me.

In his book Lance talked about his own emotional upheaval after finishing treatment, how gruelling chemotherapy was for him and how crucial support of family and friends was. He also 'remained positive' and focussed on his cure from advanced cancer. Later on, when he appeared on *Oprah*, his positivity to life and drugs appeared more like the arrogance and damaged functioning of a narcissist. However, if positivity was a door you shut on negativity, then mine was warped and let in the grey light of pessimism. Lance said that sometimes you need to support and reassure the people who are alongside you as they're scared too. Once I was home I tried this out.

How are you going? B asked, patting his stomach, knowing I suffered lingering nausea from all the drugs during the hospital stay. It was the 17th day after my first cytotoxic hit. I had constipation, as well as gut pain that felt like hands were inside me trying to untwist my bowels.

I'm okay, you know – right now I'm okay, I said. How are you, pea?

Good! B gave me a bear hug and walked away to do something.

Okay then, mister, I thought. B had his singular focus switched on, a quality I admired and envied – a laser concentration over long periods of time without awareness of anyone or anything outside that focus, usually directed towards acquiring a new skill or learning.

I thought of Armstrong's words to return the favour. I reassured my loved ones that as B and I rode the embattled River Styx that was chemotherapy, their support made a big difference.

As a family we had the luxury of being able to place everyone in different camps. B resumed work while his mother cared for Celso at his auntie's house: a beautiful 100-year-old Queenslander with a grand frontage and a welcoming, quirky interior. My father remained camped in the local hotel. My sister had flown to Darwin to see old family friends and take a series of photographs as part of her entrance portfolio to study photojournalism. After the bustle of a busy oncology ward with its beeps, regular monitoring by nurses, scheduled meal times and doctor visits, I was home alone: in quarantine. This was done in a bid to avoid a repeat of what had just happened. The luxury was not unalloyed by grief. Knowing Celso was cared for was wonderful, as was the quiet time for recovery, but being separated felt strange and straining.

Twelve days after the first cycle I'd stood in front of the vanity mirror regarding my lank hair. I was alone, because B needed to look after Celso and his feeding regimen in the quarantined house. I would never shave my head unless I had to. I wasn't one of those women who threw off their hair as part of trialling a different identity: Sinead O'Connor tough-beautiful without the feminine adornment of styled hair. I had been a forceps delivery. I have identical indentations on both sides of my skull. I figured my dented noggin would make a Frankenstein out of me. But the time had come.

I placed sheets of newspaper in the bath and leant over them. I chose a number three haircut. I worked my way from my ears inwards to try a Mohawk on top of my head before going all the way. Between each shave I'd stare into the new version of me emerging. When I finished I could feel the cool air on my scalp.

Punk, I said to myself in the mirror. The prickly hairdo was nice to rub.

In the third week after chemotherapy, when I was able to step outside, I walked to the local post office, which was nestled in the RBWH. I got many I'm-looking-at-you, trying-not-to-look-at-you stares. I had become a bona fide cancer patient.

The end of chemotherapy:
what is a life?

Considering how common illness is, how tremendous the spiritual change that it brings, how astonishing, when the lights of health go down, the undiscovered countries that are then disclosed, what wastes and deserts of the soul a slight attack of influenza brings to view, what precipices and lawns sprinkled with bright flowers a little rise of temperature reveals, what ancient and obdurate oaks are uprooted in us by the act of sickness, how we go down into the pit of death and feel the waters of annihilation close above our heads and wake thinking to find ourselves in the presence of angels and the harpers when we have a tooth out and come to the surface in the dentist's arm-chair and confuse his 'Rinse the mouth – rinse the mouth' with the greeting of the Deity stooping from the floor of Heaven to welcome us – when we think of this, as we are so frequently forced to think of it, it becomes strange indeed that illness has not taken its place with love and battle and jealousy among the prime themes of literature.

Virginia Woolf, *On Being Ill*

My guts butterflied as I walked into the day oncology unit for my second round of chemotherapy. My oncologist was not on duty that day, so I got a young stand-in, who was fine-boned and very slight. It was shocking to look at this clearly bright woman and think of her as healthy. If she covered her hair with a beanie and sat next to me in the waiting room you would mistake her for a patient immersed in her own chemotherapy regimen. Her manner was brisk. In her office we talked about how nauseated I had been with the last chemotherapy session and my hospital admission from infection. I discovered I was meant to have taken steroids before the visit, but I hadn't been told to. She decided to deliver the steroid dose intravenously before my TCH treatment.

It started out normally. I was eating a Greek salad that had raw onion in it. *Is the onion making me light-headed?* I thought, staring into the reds and greens of my salad. I was involuntarily drawing in bigger breaths of air. *I'm just anxious: calm down.* I straightened my spine against the blue padded-leather kickback chair and closed my eyes.

A nurse fitted my first hit of chemo, Taxotere, to the intravenous line replacing the steroids and saline. Okay?

I briefly opened my eyes and nodded.

Taxotere started and my breathing hammered in my chest.

Are you okay?

My eyes bugged and I shook my head. No.

The head nurse was called and a flurry of activity commenced. Put this under your tongue.

The Valium-type drug dissolved in my mouth while they fitted oxygen tubes into my nostrils and stopped all the medications going into me.

Just focus on breathing – you'll be okay, instructed the head nurse.

I focussed on her eyes. I was shaking uncontrollably again. Nurses bundled me in heated blankets and took my temperature.

They thought I'd developed what's called a 'septic shower', meaning when the nurse accessed my portacath to check my bloods in the morning some of the residual bacterial infection after my first chemotherapy hit might have got flushed back into my system. Once the reaction was under control the nurse started chemo up again. My oncologist's stand-in was reluctant to alter the dosage, which seemed the right decision, so drugs were provided to mask my stressed-out body. I later asked my oncologist what had caused the stress response and she reasoned I was likely sensitive to the steroid dose, rather than suffering from a septic shower.

Chemotherapy was more gruelling than I could have imagined – even reading and hearing the horror stories didn't prepare me for how it felt. It was the same with childbirth; no matter what women said to me there was no way of *knowing* until my body writhed with full-blown ripping contractions.

Once my body had calmed down from its shaking and my breathing returned, I distanced myself from it by closing my eyes and letting my ears lead me around the room. I overheard a conversation between an educated woman in her 50s, who was accompanied by a professional carer, and a country woman in her 60s, who had an attentive son. In my head I named the two women 'Margaret' and 'Dawn'.

Margaret: I was supposed to go last November.

Dawn: Yes … they told me this year.

She turned her head to look at Margaret. The permed hair on the back of her head was thin; her scalp was purple-pink.

Margaret: It's just statistics! Don't believe the dates.

She readjusted her Japanese print blouse.

Dawn nodded. I don't. I feel I'll be here for some time longer.

Her son bowed his head.

Margaret: Me too.

I was reminded that there were tougher cases than mine. It was a dark place, chemotherapy. A death tendril touched me. I knew I wasn't dying immediately of the disease, but the effects of the drugs in the first weeks after my two hits of chemotherapy let me know that the breast cancer business was deadly serious.

There was another side to being ill too. There were heightened thoughts and feelings, like the sadness of finally understanding some of what my mother had faced when she was ill. I hadn't had the foresight to record her voice.

In my chemotherapy haze I stood back from the normal running of life. I observed others without experiencing the fast rush of get-to-work adrenaline. The comings and goings of daily routine were slowed down so that I noticed where my feet fell.

My mind kept returning to the idea of myself as a phoenix rising out of the ashes of my mother's death, out of a cancer death. As I turned on my side to get relief from a constipated belly, the bony hips leaping out of my flesh were my mother's. I was inside the last days of my mother's life; I witnessed her frame inside mine and mine inside hers.

When my mother went into a coma the nurse put her into an adult nappy. Her best friend, Tess, and I rubbed oil into the sagging skin on Mum's stick legs. We spoke to her as if she was conscious in the room and to reassure her she wasn't alone, though she was alone in her mind. If hearing was the last sense to go then she knew of our presence.

My mother's breast cancer was different from mine. She had lobular early-stage invasive breast cancer that was positive to oestrogen and progesterone. I remembered her getting the news that she was HER2 negative. The details were hazy, but I was driving her somewhere – either back to the Northern Rivers after seeing her overloaded and unavailable oncologist in Brisbane or on our way to the beach for a walk. When I visited, Mum always preferred it if I drove, and went up to the till to pay in cafés with her money. My mother had an innate shyness and a reclusive nature even though her academic life required her to speak in front of people and educate others. She often said, I'd love to live in a lighthouse. She had a framed picture of a man standing outside the bottom of his lighthouse with the one red door closed behind him. A heaving ocean with a wave that only sailors see has spilt around the structure and is caught at the moment it is about to return, merge and possibly swamp him. You can't see how he'll get out of the way of this wave.

It stung to recall our chats and driving times. We used to talk so openly on drives, our eyes to the front and our emotions easy. The loss felt even greater after the heightened intimacy of the car in the last few months of Mum's life, as I drove her to regular shots of palliative chemo.

A dragged-down heart, similar in feeling to when I was hospitalised after my first chemotherapy session, was the best expression I could find to cover the loss of conversations with my mother about our favourite authors, books and theories. In the year I cared for her full time our conversations had no time for meandering through texts or our shared past stories. The ever present scorched our lives so fiercely; I was holding onto the hours with sharpened nails, and what required attention: medical, emotional and legal.

I can't get Herceptin the miracle drug, Mum said after ending the call with her oncologist – the one whose nameplate sat next to my future oncologist's in Wesley Hospital private rooms.

Why not?

It's only for a particular kind of cancer. Mum sighed, and then shrugged her shoulders, keeping her eyes to the front. The positive side of that is Herceptin treats a more aggressive cancer, which I haven't got.

This was the cancer waiting for me four years later.

That's good. You don't want an aggressive cancer, I replied without thinking.

No, it's just I was kind of hoping to get the drug as it works really well at keeping it away. Mum scrunched her nose up and looked over at me.

Some cost for having a nasty C. Better to keep the one you've got.

I didn't know what Mum was talking about at the time. The name of the HER2 protein didn't register, only the drug, Herceptin. I received Herceptin with each chemotherapy dose and continued to get IV shots of it every three weeks for eight months post-chemo. It didn't make me ill like chemo, and this alone would have been a real positive for Mum – something she would have considered if she had been HER2 positive, like me.

I held such different views of Mum's decisions and thinking around cancer care after I was diagnosed. What I thought were clear-eyed opinions weren't. I believe now that fear informed her choices more than an understanding of the reality of cancer in her breast and the medical intervention required to eradicate it from her body. Maybe Mum's initial rejection of chemotherapy drugs but acceptance of Herceptin as an option was another way of skirting around the edges of conventional medicine. She was comfortable using medicine's well-researched drugs without the terror of chemo's side effects: a half-in, half-out strategy. After my own diagnosis and reading up on my particular kind of breast cancer I had to acknowledge that my mother would have been profoundly disappointed after hearing her HER2 status was negative.

Sentinel node biopsies were in their infancy in 1996, so she didn't have that option; only the full removal of lymph nodes under her arm and radiotherapy were offered, which would have likely left her with lymphedema (build-up of lymph fluid that would lead to swelling in the arms), so she'd had a lumpectomy only. The treating doctor suggested radiotherapy on top of surgery, but my mother refused it on the grounds that it hardened the breast tissue and could compromise healing, plus if it returned in that breast after radiotherapy a mastectomy would likely be the only option instead of another lumpectomy. She took the other route. The one that failed her. I only understood the degree to which she hung onto the chance of new cancer treatments *in light* of my now-lived experience.

By the third round of my chemo I had more of an idea of how to handle the anti-emetics and get through the nausea. It took approximately three to four hours to deliver my chemotherapy so the oncology nurses offered me a bed to lie down upon, usually near large windows that had metal shutters sandwiched between their panes of glass to make them dust free, and a warm blanket for my shrinking body.

By this stage in my treatment some form of scattered rhythm had formed: after the first week of ill health and extreme side effects from chemo, a glimmer of normality would return for the remaining two weeks. In these weeks, I cared full time for my son without assistance, and my health returned in a way I recognised wasn't full health, but a functional health where I ran my life without a fogged brain and nausea weighing my movements to a snail's pace.

Supine on my white bed I looked around and took in everyone plugged into their chemicals. It was a plain hospital room but held so much concentrated humanity. The atmosphere of many nurses, caring family members and visiting doctors in plain clothes made the feeling of being cared for sharper for me. The room was awash with cancer patients but we were safer from the disease than at any other time since diagnosis.

A corridor away a nameless, faceless chemist read our vital statistics and mixed a chemo-intoxicant tailored to us. Each of us sat with the slow drip of hope that what we were going through would cure us.

Plugged into my chemical infusion I heard soulful music by Joni Mitchell playing on another patient's CD player. The patient was Mum's age. I heard my mother talking again.

I spent most of my science degree in my room painting, Mum would say when we wandered into conversation about the life she had before me. As a post–World War II English baby Mum benefitted from a free and supported education – a saviour for bright working-class people.

I wasn't allowed to study some of the harder sciences as a woman, said Mum. So I did biology, zoology and botany … the stupid things women had to fight to do. In 1960s Sheffield women in chemistry laboratories had to wear stockings and a skirt. I addressed the union, got a petition going and was then granted permission to enter the classroom wearing protective slacks like the men. The noxious fumes melted our nylon stockings off anyway.

I really missed my mother that day – and any day I remembered her feisty nature and her campaigns for women's rights. She too was once a young woman with a life ahead of her.

My son would never meet the grandmother who adored him even before he was conceived. A month before Mum died she wrote a letter to her grandchildren. When we talked of my future we imagined I'd have two children, not one. In her letter she told the imaginary two children of my future how to make a paper mat, a lesson she'd learnt from her time living in Nigeria. In the early 1970s my mother was in voluntary service abroad, teaching science and English in a hut full of children of all ages. In the A4 exercise book Mum wrote in for her grandchildren she said:

> … it is best – I think I have learnt – not to make your mind up that only <u>one</u> thing is right. Actually the world is always changing and so are you – so each day, each moment is the time to decide what is right then.

Here is a poem I wrote about all that:

The Meaning of Life

The meaning of life is really quite simple
One minute you're up –
The next you're a pimple.
It ain't that 'they' hate you,
And it isn't all fate
It's just that the world's fishing
And you are the bait!

My mother was an only child because she was adopted and her adoptive parents couldn't afford to have any more children. I was an only child because my mother and father separated within a year of my birth and my mother never had the kind of stable relationship again that would have allowed for another child, and she wasn't in a financial situation where she could raise two children as a sole parent and give them the kind of life she'd want for them. I shone as an only child of an adoring single mother. My father was also an only child, because allegedly his parents only ever conceived once. I too will have one child – to conceive and bear another child would be to play Russian roulette with my oestrogen. Too much woman can kill you, I now knew.

Three generations of only children whose parents wanted more.

Throughout my experience of breast cancer I read about other people's journeys, for want of a better word, with cancer. The idea of the self is stripped, ripped, dissolved when you're going through chemotherapy. What you once did is no longer; what you are is surviving day by day, running the gauntlet as ghosts of the dead reach out to trip you up. Come die with us, they say.

The Bronx-born memoirist Vivian Gornick talked of the idea of self – the one that is shaped for the reader as a story progresses – as the organising principle of good memoir. In *The Situation and the Story: The Art of Personal Narrative*, she writes that the question being asked in memoir is: *'Who am I?' Who exactly is this 'I' upon whom turns the significance of this story-taken-directly-from-life? On that question the writer of memoir must deliver. Not with an answer but with depth of inquiry.*

The awareness of even having a self was challenging during this period.

My mother, alive and dead, helped me to access my selfhood. My mother's mothering gave direction – shaped my life – as my devotional love for my son was shaping his life. She taught me to examine my actions and reactions. I didn't always welcome this training in self-assessment. I didn't always like what I saw.

Underneath our raised Queenslander were boxes of memorabilia. In one of my clear-outs I picked up an old diary of my mother's and opened it. Mum's familiar fast-flowing script was there. It travelled at 45 degrees across lined pages and turned into thought bubbles and spidery plans. *I must stop letting Josie take responsibility for my life and in turn stop her turning to me to tell her what to do*, she'd written. I shut the black A4 diary and dropped it like a hot potato. It fell onto the dusty concrete.

The kind of house I lived in was typical for our inner-city suburb. Herston sits like a retro chair beside the modern sofa that is Kelvin Grove: a suburb of students, renovators and people inhabiting old buildings that've seen too much of life. Herston's elegantly shaped Queenslanders recall a time when the backyard fence wasn't visible from the back door. A 100-year flood came to the suburb in 1974, and then again 37 years later in 2011 (early for its century). When the floods burst the banks in the city and surrounding suburbs it went on to create an inland tsunami, changing many people's lives: from short-term blackouts to deaths in the family.

Most homes in Herston sat on high stilts and their occupants lived on the top floor, due to its history of going under. Those who had dared to build in their underfloor space to make a cheap third or fourth bedroom would risk losing everything in it to a mud surge in the 2011 floods.

When I witnessed another builder's truck outside a neighbour's home I heard the experienced builder with scars on the back of his hands say: Stuff the termite-caps, you try fishbowl proofing an entire floor, mate.

My mother had been right. I'd relied on her as the final judge on my decisions. Instead of studying sciences alongside psychology with a secret goal of switching to medicine later, I took women's studies on my mother's advice. This sliding-doors moment wasn't her responsibility, but mine. I wasn't honest with her or myself. We're each our own best expert, I guess. We know the answers to our questions, even if we refuse to acknowledge it.

This revelation hung in the dull air of under-the-house. My heart was beating fast. I picked up the book again and tried another page. Mum talked of being lost, so very lost. This was the darker side of mothering my mother: that deep, cellular task of being responsible for her during my life and until her death.

The truth of this light-bulb moment of my mother and our co-dependency was similar to Gornick's, but with Gornick she often hated her mother whereas I always loved mine.

In Gornick's *Fierce Attachments*, she recounts how her mother is absorbed in her own grief after the sudden death at 46 of her adored husband, her raison d'être. The bubble of her mother's grief played out for the rest of Gornick's childhood and adulthood. The mother's heightened state of pain, acted out daily in long periods on the couch, whittled her life away in depression – smothering Gornick's lived life with a mother who existed in abstraction. Decades later, they would end up walking through Manhattan together, their conversations filled in turn with laughter or fierce anger. They would discover things about each other, like the time they both spoke about the abortions they'd had. Gornick's mother had had three during the Depression. After one, she'd woken from the anaesthetic delivered by a low-grade doctor in a basement apartment with his penis in her hand.

I wanted to be rid of my mother's burdening book. Its personal, deeply internal, anguished words were my mother's and not mine to read. Mum never presented herself as inviolable to me but I thought of her that way anyway. I walked outside and threw the book into the recycling bin.

The first thing I did on diagnosis was reach out to learn what to do from women who had survived breast cancer, not died from it like my mother had. I contacted the Choices Cancer Support Centre, who put me in touch with another woman around my age who was a few steps ahead in her cancer treatments. Others' stories were so vital, experiences I could deeply relate to.

With three friends I formed a support group called the Right Wingers, because we all had breast cancer in the right breast, and planned to have a mastectomy (or had had one already). I also attended Choices' support group for young women with breast cancer. For our Christmas in July night I'd sat near two other women my age, also with only one child, who'd similarly made the decision not to tempt Ms Oestrogen and conceive again.

The room was plain and made specifically for groups coming for dinner. We had a choice of turkey or chicken. I chose turkey, which was dry, but I wasn't there for the meal. All the women's eyes around the table were bright and alert to what the others were saying.

Opposite me was a woman who'd finished treatment a year before, proudly showing pictures of her attractive bald head. She was a surgical nurse and acted as our interpreter for the medical lingo of breast cancer pathology. To my left was an active breast cancer advocate who'd waved goodbye to cancer 22 years before. She said, At the time I thought I would be dead in a year, so I didn't want to bother with building an extension to our deck. It remains unbuilt all these years later.

The good-news story of the evening was a woman diagnosed seven years prior with oestrogen-positive breast cancer whose fertility eventually kicked back in during her late 30s. It allowed her to have the children she'd always wanted (she remained cancer free).

Stories like hers placed a question mark on my decision not to have another child, but a doctor's words always returned to match my own concerns. If your cancer is oestrogen positive, he'd said, why would you flood your body with the hormone through pregnancy?

For women going through breast cancer treatments in Brisbane there was an active community of support. Apart from Choices, public hospitals offered social workers, psychologists and psychiatrists, and I could also access a breast clinic at Mater Private, where I went for my surgeries. In these clinics you get assigned a breast care nurse who takes your drains out after operations and is available to keep an eye on you post-operatively.

During chemotherapy, my mood dipped and rose, and I went to a hospital-based psychologist. She did a mapping-out technique where I could step back and do a life review. It helped me to see the situation more clearly and some possible ways out of it: that chemo would end, better health would come, and which personal capabilities I could draw upon to meet Celso's needs. After my designated six visits the psychologist referred me to a psychiatrist who specialised in breast cancer care. The psychiatrist visited me on chemo days so I didn't have to make a separate appointment. Once the anti-depressants, prescribed for depression and to reduce hot flushes, elevated then evened out my mood, I could function well.

Both of these professionals were free and based in the public hospital system. I would dip and rise again, but I had the mechanics at hand to get myself mentally competent when required.

The breast care nurses I saw were attached to the Chicks in Pink charity, part of the Mater Private hospital. They raised funds for many things, for example bras for women after mastectomies, and portable DVD players for women in hospital. One fateful day my breast care nurse called at just the right time. I was sinking that day. At this stage Celso had no diagnosis but merely a collection of medical problems including gastro-oesophageal reflux disease, food refusal and delayed speech. He was going through a period of waking up and vomiting at 2 a.m., and remaining awake for several hours. He wouldn't settle himself in the cot and needed to be held and soothed the entire time. He was still nasogastrically fed and required his nose tape changed every two days, which he fought, screaming throughout. B's and my days were filled with darkness. B called it *eating cardboard*.

How are you going? my breast care nurse asked.

Okay, I lied. Tears sprang up into my eyes and I tried not to show them in my voice.

What's happening for you at the moment?

Well ... I said and proceeded to unravel what was going on and the depression that was riding my back at the time.

Oh, I'm so sorry I didn't call earlier. I'm so glad I called today, because ...

And my breast care nurse explained that she would arrange some private funding from the breast clinic for a nanny. The very weekend before calling me she'd met some women she knew (I never found out their names) who'd put on a successful fundraiser and wanted to give a portion of money directly to a woman with breast cancer in a difficult situation. Well, all us cancer patients were. But I was officially on a tricky, muddy tightrope of a path with a son whose path was just as tricky and muddy, so they donated the money to us. B and I were able to juggle B's relatives and our friends around professional nannies so that for the first week of each chemotherapy round, when I was immersed in my toxic haze, B could work if he wished to and I could rest.

I did, after all, have some guardian angels.

After years of hard work, Celso's path did end up smoothing out. I tried all the occupational therapists, dieticians, speech therapists and the evidence-based desensitisation tricks of their trades. Only physiotherapists' advice helped. That treatment, plus commencing the Son-Rise process, meant that, after three-and-a-half years of not eating and in the midst of somehow getting salmonella poisoning, Celso pointed to the bottle of electrolyte hooked onto the mobile IV pole that followed him everywhere.

You want some of this, darling? I asked.

Celso pointed. I quickly put some into a sippy cup. The salty taste caused him to cough, but he appeared keen. I replaced the green fluorescent liquid with water and he allowed some into his mouth, then dribbled the rest down his chin.

Within half an hour he'd tried a baby's squeeze tube of organic mushed-up food. He had a bath to cool his temperature down, sitting on a stool because his bottom was sore from diarrhoea. His pale face and the dark shadows under his eyes made his lips appear lipstick red. Once out of the bath and wrapped up in a towel he dared tasting more on a spoon – tongue darting out.

He had eaten and drunk nothing since he was seven weeks old, when the nasogastric tube went in, but in 24 hours he was nibbling a soft Anzac biscuit, sipping water (albeit with his tongue positioned out the side of the cup), and squeezing baby food into his mouth. To reinforce this he searched hungrily for food words in his books, getting me to say out loud all their names: tomato, sandwich, ice cream.

My son and I followed parallel paths through the medical system: me to treat a known cancer and him to find out what to treat.

The fourth round was on 28 August.

Nausea. How I hated nausea. It destabilised me like nothing else. It came on and I was lost in Bass Strait, clinging to a life raft, praying for a passing ship to lift me off and away from the wet, cold ordeal.

Friday was chemotherapy day. I had a routine. I'd walk up to the day oncology unit, sign myself in at the front desk then walk around to the nurse, a kind woman who could be stern when required. I let her know I was there waiting for my oncologist appointment then chemotherapy. Before either of these things happened I'd get my bloods taken via my portacath to check if I had enough oxygen in my red blood cells and if my white cell count was keeping up, among other things. My Fridays started around 7 a.m. and finished late afternoon. I enjoyed these days – not for the snake oil shunted into my heart but for having a day completely to myself, knowing my son was well cared for by someone else. Invariably I wasn't sick yet so could revel in the time alone: I wasn't a mother, I wasn't a partner, I was my other self – a woman going through breast cancer treatment with an internal life.

Once, when I was waiting to see my oncologist before going in to receive treatment, I sat in front of a low table with outdated women's magazines and peered around the packed waiting room. I had Randy Pausch's *The Last Lecture* in my hand. He was a computer science lecturer at a prestigious American university and delivered a talk to his students on living that turned into a book. I wanted to read his take on setting goals to achieve your childhood dreams. But I didn't have the space in my head to read or take in the words. A woman in her late 50s was brought into the waiting room in a wheelchair. It appeared she'd come straight down from the oncology ward. She was shaking. Her arms and legs were thin. And she had the unmistakeable grey soft curls of hair growing back after chemotherapy. She was vulnerable and ill. All really sick cancer patients reminded the rest of us who walked into the day unit how cancer could suck the body in and leave it deathly. It was scary to behold, but also humbling. She reminded me of my mother in her final days at the John Flynn Private Hospital on the Gold Coast.

My mother had her own room and bathroom at John Flynn. Near her end, when I stayed close by, I returned in the evenings to put her to bed. Part of her nightly routine was to clean her teeth properly, have an English bath, pat on some talcum powder and likely attempt the toilet. During these occasions she'd rest her head on my stomach from her position on the toilet seat and we'd talk. Her hair was grey with soft curls. Her arms and legs were thin and shaky. She was ill and dying. In fact, we didn't know she was so close to death then.

In the first week or so she said, I feel guilty taking up this whole room. What if the nurses think I'm faking it?

Mum was doing well then: alert, feeling okay, in good spirits. We regarded her stay as a private-health-funded hotel room while B and I prepared our new home for Mum to join us. I was organising Karuna, a Buddhist hospice service that provided outreach to the north side of Brisbane, to assist us in caring for Mum there in our home. I was also organising the transport of her possessions from her house in Lismore, which we'd sold.

The drive between Brisbane and John Flynn was about an hour and a half one way. Mum was relaxed with the professional nurses and doctors in a way she couldn't be with me as her carer. The meals, though not brilliant, were delivered routinely. At the end institutionalisation wasn't such a negative for a woman who had more important things to worry about, like living within a dying body without being in extremis. My mother could 'relax' knowing she was medically contained. When I was caring for her full time, she'd have to remind me if I'd missed one of her pain medications through exhaustion, as there was no one else overseeing the schedule.

My own treatment was also made easier by the help I received from others. My fourth chemo session went smoothly and I handled the post-chemo body meltdown well. I wished that this would be the case for my remaining chemo regimen, but it wasn't.

My fifth chemo session was hell. Everything seemed to go awry. Good friends, Sara and Ian, from over the border in Mullumbimby, were with us to care for Celso, so B could care for me. They were classical musicians, book and language lovers with a compassion for others not found in many people. They had formed friendships with Iranian and Afghan refugees, and they'd visited their friends' families in Iran and provided financial assistance to mothers left behind in Afghanistan.

They were with us for the four days. They did the night shift with Celso so B and I could rest. But come Sunday, things weren't looking so good for Celso. He was red-faced with a fever, he had diarrhoea and did a lot of vomiting, and he was floppy. The locum was concerned about swine flu (again), which was still running its course through Queensland, alongside another animal virus, the deadly Hendra virus.

Both my son and I were put on Tamiflu antibiotics, which were nasty for the stomach, until we could get checked by our GP. B didn't get the Tamiflu, though he was quickly sick too. By the time the virus really kicked in we were up like ghouls bumping around the house throughout the entire night. B was in the toilet with the flu or whatever it was, bent over. I tried to help him by getting some water, so I tiptoed into the kitchen to get a glass, past Sara asleep on her made-up bed on the dining room floor. I fumbled around in the cupboard and smashed a champagne glass.

Sara was up.

Then Ian was up, changing my son's diarrhoea nappies. Celso was up too. He had a fever, was projectile vomiting like his father – and crotchety. When Celso got tired or wasn't happy he rubbed at his eyes and at the tape on his face, which held his tube in. His scratching led to him pulling part of his tube out. After this occurred, all adults were up trying to settle Celso, putting his tube back down, and fixing his tape to his skin. Ian and Sara had to supervise both my partner's and son's health and check they weren't getting worse. Later on when our friends returned home they too got a dose of the norovirus.

Come the following Tuesday our son was hospitalised for two days at the Royal Children's Hospital. I couldn't go near him because of my low immunity, though I had the G-CSF injections on board forcing my bones to generate more white blood cells. B was exhausted and close to collapse. We had nannies, paid for by the Mater's Chicks in Pink, stay overnight with him at the hospital so B could get some sleep. Our son was put on electrolytes and made a quick recovery.

But even those dark days passed. One morning the week after, I heard B call to me from the dining room. Can you get a bib? I'm trying to tempt Celso with some yoghurt.

I was bent over putting on pyjama bottoms in our bedroom. I grabbed a pin-bib and hobbled out. Leant over B and tried to fit it around his neck. B gave me an *Is this a joke?* look.

The bib reached his ears. Oops, you're not Celso. I turned around and fitted Celso with it instead. He beamed up at me and gurgled. Even through his physical difficulties Celso was such a sweet little boy.

He didn't appear to notice his mother no longer had hair or wore blue cotton beanies. He'd walk over to yellow ducks I'd lined up on the coffee table and swat them off – laughing open-mouthed with delight. He knew how to *do* joy: staring out at the world around him with fingers outstretched to touch something new – sucking into his world the day's rays and all its looming oddities.

Various doctors from psychiatrists to oncologists have talked about how cancer patients find the end of chemotherapy treatment the hardest part of it. When the cancer-kicking drugs are over, you are faced with life post-treatment and a new horizon with questions: Will my cancer return? Am I cured? Am I safe?

No one can answer these. The only comfort of chemotherapy is that you're protected from carcinoma attacking your body, with a Molotov cocktail of drugs ready to smite any raised malignant head. There is security in chemotherapy.

The day after I finished my treatment I lay on my bed at home and took in the room's dimensions: three metres by four. The blind's wooden slats were closed. The curtain was drawn to keep out the vibrant spring sun, and the small sleep-out attached to the room let in a diffuse light. The high ceiling moulds were ornate and the light hung down loosely with a long-lasting fluorescent bulb protruding from a conical glass lampshade. The shadows drew my slow attention. Underneath the room's original floorboards, a breezeway kept the house cool. It was the middle of the day and I was unable to move or drink: just inert with my head absorbed by the pillow, and the duvet covering my legs. My son babbled bubba speak somewhere in the house to our German-banker nanny, whose husband was an engineer working a diamond-encrusted underground boring machine to make way for a freeway tunnel. My weight was dropping rapidly. For four days after the final chemo session I ate nothing apart from dry Jatz crackers.

I spent a week in bed staring at my hips protruding from my 51-kilogram frame. My gut didn't work brilliantly, so there was internal pain. I was constipated on some days and greeted with diarrhoea on others. The skin around my fingernails was split like a dry creek bed and my haemoglobin levels needed to be higher so that I wasn't at risk of constant anaemia. When it became too much I watched episodes of *The West Wing*'s season one lying side-on in my bed. I finished the entire season.

I remained in an ill-chemical haze for one week. I didn't think I could keep going, being that unwell. I wanted to re-read *The Cure for Death by Lightning* about a Coyote spirit that tries to marry a local farm girl, 15-year-old Beth. Beth overcomes self-harming to turn the hunter into the hunted and the bad spirit flees. Gail Anderson-Dargatz's mythological quest set in Canada was just what I needed – its tale of warding off evil fitted my daily conversation with cancer, my evil Coyote – but I had no energy to engage with it.

My son's godmother, Ngaire, returned to spend a week with us for my last chemo session. Ngaire was a retired Canberran college teacher of sociology and psychology. She did night shifts caring for our son, cooked lovely meals and was in all manners a gorgeous presence.

On her last night with us she shouted us takeaway fish and chips. The fish was grilled, and the chips were not that many. However, a funny thing happened on their way down my digestive tract. Within half an hour of eating, my stomach rose and rose until it formed the shape of a semi-deflated football. I was alarmed, but also felt like vomiting and was in a bit of discomfort. It expelled itself in the bathroom – several times. Rise – expel – rise again. My entire meal went down the Brisbane underground sewage system.

I put this down to the fact that chemo's effects were cumulative and the fast-growing cells in my stomach and other places didn't like fat getting in the way, or quite simply couldn't digest fat any longer. As I lay down on the bed after my toilet visit I remembered a cancer pamphlet in the preparation room I walked around in before my first chemotherapy session, advising patients to avoid fried foods because they were too harsh for a chemo patient's stomach, as well as not being so healthy. I decided on the spot that I was like a dog, but instead of not being able to digest chocolate I couldn't digest chips. I swore I'd never eat chips again, and haven't.

People often asked me what the chemicals did to my sense of taste. It's a little like brushing your teeth with double-strength mint toothpaste, then grabbing cold strawberries fresh out of the fridge and popping them in your mouth; you're hopeful of something tasting sweet but it doesn't. More like aluminium foil on teeth fillings.

Three weeks after chemotherapy my hair sprouted through my scalp. I no longer had a flushed face from the steroids. I remained whacked with tiredness but not so badly it rocked my world. I no longer experienced intense nausea or food aversion. The metallic twang faded from my mouth.

The more extreme side effects from my chemo cocktail diminished fairly quickly. The residual effects of Taxotere were muscle fatigue and anaemia. From Carboplatin you can get peripheral neuropathy (numbness and tingling of the extremities), which can affect your ability to walk. This disappeared, but returned when I started cycling for more than an hour. I was so happy that the dreaded chemo times were over and the next phase was in full swing that I barely considered these side effects. With my chemical romance came some other, not-too-serious side effects. My chemo flatulence alone could have cleared the Opera House of its guests and possibly some of its tiles.

I finished chemotherapy in October and once the anxiety and depression lifted I looked forward to the victory lap we'd planned around the South Island of New Zealand the following month.

I had a new oncologist as the first one was on maternity leave, having had a baby boy. My new oncologist spoke quickly and could go off on quick tangents of thought. It was like her rapid-firing brain had so much processing going on that sometimes thoughts fell out of her mouth into conversation. She'd come to Brisbane from Sydney and was searching for a Queenslander to make her stay more permanent. I clicked easily with her. I wasn't good enough on the piano, she said during an oncology visit. She'd once attended the conservatory of music, but after giving up classical piano she went into medicine.

Patients generally expect chemotherapy will make them infertile – it often does. Three weeks after I finished, though, a period arrived. I told my new oncologist.

I didn't think we'd need to start Zoladex so quickly, but we do, she said. Your oestrogen levels have risen enough to cause menstruation, so we'll need to send you into menopause to reduce your risk of breast cancer returning.

Zoladex is a monthly injection that sends you into a chemical menopause (it's also used to chemically castrate men). It basically visits your ovaries and says, Hiya, girls, sorry about this but there'll be no more eggs from you, and switches them off like a handy plumber. I had just experienced my last period, ever.

The following week I sat again in a puffy blue remote-controllable chair in the day oncology unit. This time instead of exposing my portacath to a chemo needle I exposed my belly to a needle the size of a pen. The nurse did something clever when she administered my first Zoladex injection. First, she injected a local anaesthetic just under my skin to form a small bump, which stung a bit. Then she got the Zoladex needle – Don't look, she said, but I did – and she injected a pellet-sized deposit of chemical into the bump so it wouldn't hurt. Which it didn't. The pellet's contents dispersed over four weeks, and then I'd get another hit. The plan was to do this every month until I was near the normal age to be post-menopausal – 15 years away.

Other women warned me that when you're sent into a sudden menopause, bad moods can come on. No. Anger came on. I returned from shopping for dinner one afternoon – a healthy meal of salmon fillet, steamed vegetables and rice – with my temper boiling.

I got out the steamer and cleared away breakfast plates and crumbs off the bench top. I wrung out the damp cloth and placed it on a hook to dry. The groceries were poking through the clear plastic bag, as I'd forgotten my green bags. This was my 'office', in which I cleaned, cooked, and organised every day. I gripped the sink with both hands. My life was going to pot: I was living the life of the meek; I couldn't stand being a house queen anymore; and I wanted someone else to look after my son while I returned to meaningful work. Full stop. But wait! I didn't have work to return to; I was a 35-year-old loser. And on it went. My body was ramrod stiff but my eyes darted around, searching for an answer in my bag, out of the radio, out the window. Depression was again kicking my front teeth in.

Memory: will my relationship cope?

My dreams are going through their death flurries ... I thought they were all safely buried, but sometimes they stir in their grave, making my heartstrings twinge. I mean no particular dream, you understand, but the whole radiant flock of them together – with their rainbow wings, iridescent, bright, soaring, glorious, sublime. They are dying before the steel javelins and arrows of a world of Time and Money.

Barbara Follett, *Barbara*

I had no energy. It was draining down the plughole, the bath water chasing it down. The noise of it outdid Celso's vocal protests. At this point his large, washable change table stood in the nook just outside our bathroom. The nook had four doors off it, leading to our bedroom, the bathroom, Celso's room and the lounge room. A phone line ran up the side of the wall beside four semi-circular wooden shelves. We used these shelves for baby stuff: wipes and nappy rash creams. To get Celso from the bath to the change table took two steps.

On the table, he kicked his legs into my stomach. His pudgy, working feet occasionally kicked my caesarean scar, which made me wince and draw my hips away. From the change table to his room took four steps.

Everyone was telling me that a regular sleeping pattern was 'best for baby, best for parent'. I had commenced putting my son down two hours before. He was still crying. Inconsolable. We both were. My son writhed in my arms. His eyes were watering. He needed to sleep. I did too; I was sinking. The older he got the more likely it appeared that he had a developmental delay and God knew what else. This was before any diagnoses, before I found life-altering programs and the right physical therapy. He wouldn't eat food. I had to get nutrients into him with a special formula made by a Dutch pharmaceutical company and shipped up from Sydney. He was still nasogastrically fed; a tube went up his nose, down his oesophagus and into his stomach. I needed to sleep. He needed to sleep. I wanted out of cancer. I wanted out of mothering. I wished my son wasn't this child. I wanted him without special needs. If only we'd conceived another night. A different egg and sperm would've mixed another baby – a normal, healthy baby. But I still wanted that baby as this baby. Just a normal version.

A Texan yogi in *Eat, Pray, Love* gave Elizabeth Gilbert good advice when he said that if you couldn't control your mind you were in trouble.

I was in deep trouble.

Depression had come home to roost, to ride my back. All the doubts rushed in. What was I doing trying to write a young adult novel as part of my master's? This wouldn't work. I wasn't a writer. When I opened books and read the author's bio it usually went:

Mary Stage wrote *The Luck of Beauty* at 25. It was an instant bestseller. She was a journalist with *The Times* before she wrote said novel. Her second novel won the Orange Prize for Fiction. Her third book, a work of non-fiction, is ritually on the contemporary classics list in all good universities. She resides with her Italian husband, Pietro, a doctor for Médecins Sans Frontières and ex-model, in Milan with their fraternal twins Cute and Cuter. They divide their time between Western Europe, New York and Ireland.

Due to Ms Stage's success she now wrote full time. Her husband could support her anyway because he was a former highly paid clothes hanger and current well-paid doctor. Her breasts weren't sagging (… or coming off) as she was a freak of nature but in a good way. Ms Stage didn't need to wax her bikini line (hair just didn't grow there, man), clean the bathroom, do the shopping, cook meals or spend all her creative energy on her children due to having a fairy doppelganger who spared her the trouble.

I was not like this. Not one little bit.

Brisbane summer was twirling her full skirt and flashing everyone with her naked brilliance. Here, when you step outside the home, your pupils constrict so sharply that you walk around with tunnel vision for a minute.

My hormones or lack of them made me grumpy under the oppressive warmth of Brisbane's wet armpit hug. Or, as the literature for women taking Zoladex says, *Mood changes are common.*

I was bathing Celso, leaning my arms on the porcelain edge of the bath, and ruminating. B was watching ABC iView in the other room. *Yeah, just suck up that TV, arsehole, crisps in hand with nothing to do.*

I fumbled something and it dropped to the ground. For fuck's sake! sprang out of my mouth.

B rushed in. Are you all right?

I get tired too, you know, I blared into his face.

Okay. He was wounded.

I smoothed down Celso's hair and stood up. B took over washing him.

I stormed into our room and crashed onto the four-poster bed, exhausted.

After B put Celso to bed he walked into our room. I looked up at him.

Sorry, I didn't mean it, pea, I said, feeling like five kinds of poo.

It's okay. He shrugged, then made a face. I understand.

I love B down to his mitochondria, but jab me with Zoladex and watch sparks fly. The heat from my menopausal hot flushes pressed tight upon my skin. I was claustrophobic, uncomfortable, red and sweating. I was murderous under The Menopause, and my burgeoning depression left no room for fun.

Menopause dries you up. Oestrogen is a great lubricator of the vagina, joints, skin and brain. Part of going into menopause to protect myself from cancer was negotiating a body with plummeting oestrogen levels. To help the Zoladex keep my oestrogen level down I took a pill – Arimidex – alongside high doses of Vitamin D and calcium. This was all to help my body pretend it was in its 50s or 60s. Once I'd lost the puffiness of the steroids I'd taken during treatment, my forehead resembled a ploughed field.

Breast tissue contains fat cells. Fat is considered the third ovary because it still produces oestrogen after oophorectomy. When science writer Florence Williams found substances similar to cannabis in her breast milk she delved into the history of the human breast. Endocannabinoids regulate a baby's intake of their mother's breast milk. One of the possible reasons for obesity in formula-fed babies could be the lack of hormones to regulate their appetite. Williams discovered that breasts also absorb chemicals such as fire retardants sprayed onto sofa foam.

Breasts absorb but they also create. Arimidex leaches my fat of oestrogen by being an aromatase inhibitor. Aromatase is an enzyme responsible for converting androgens ('male' hormones, like testosterone) into oestrogen. In breast tissue, aromatase is normally regulated, but when it's not, you get hormone-receptor-positive breast cancer.

In menopause many women worldwide take synthetic oestrogens to overcome their natural relinquishing of it at menopause. Williams explored this phenomenon in *Breasts: A Natural and Unnatural History*. She wrote: *By 1992, Premarin (the name stands for pregnant mare urine) was one of the most widely prescribed drugs in America, given to 11 million menopausal women and earning its happy makers nearly $2 billion a year. To create the unprecedented demand, drug companies and physicians appealed to women's vanity and reason, essentially inventing a new pathology called menopause in the same way the surgeons had invented one called micromastia, for small breasts.*

When I went through menopause instantly and younger than I would have naturally, I realised what it must be like for older women – for those no longer seen as being sexual or attractive to men (in a society that tells us that's one of the most important ways a woman can be valuable). I was distanced from my true age, which didn't bother me as I wanted to do other things like survive and write. But there was one major aspect of menopause that made me pause in my breast cancer treatment regime.

After chemotherapy my brain behaved very strangely indeed. I wanted an apple but asked for an orange. I misplaced my son's first two pairs of proper leather shoes. I left things on top of cars: one week, I drove around the suburb with my lost mobile phone stuck to the roof. I only noticed its presence when I headed out the door and spotted it on the car instead of in my handbag.

When Celso came into the world my memory for names and lists fell away through sheer exhaustion. With chemotherapy my ability to retain recent events, dates, times and appointments had not so much fallen away as been buried by a pile driver. I often walked into a room and stood still, waiting for my brain to catch up and remind me why I was there. I'd go through possible reasons: get Celso's meds, ring and make an appointment with X, organise weekend get-together, call someone back, put on washing, recall own name. It could take anywhere between five minutes and a couple of hours for the reason to spring back into my mind.

I declared myself the human goldfish. It was as if the drugs created a barrier that held my short-term memories at bay: in effect damming them. As the chemicals leached slowly from my body the ability to retain information and short-term recall of events returned a little.

It was the same with old dreams and memories; the damming process let whatever flowed closest to the filter inlet in my memory pipe pour out. I was a ten-year-old, aglow with warmth as I walked the high path back in Sydney's north shore suburb Cremorne Point. I was three, reaching up to pluck a seed out of the tall sunflowers around the fence of my crèche, still in England on the grounds of Mum's university.

I was 22 with my right cheek rested against the cool quartzite sandstone of an Arapiles climbing crag. Arapiles is a mass of rock in Victoria that sits among vast wheat fields and resembles Uluru. I was on the 'Have a good flight' wall: a slab of rock 15 minutes' walk up from the bottom of a series of outcrops. I was about to pull through the crux of the climb. My heart was audibly thumping against my chest; two far better climbers were watching (one was my then boyfriend, the other was my future boyfriend).

Is that the sound of her heart? asked future boyfriend.

The current boyfriend (belaying me) kindly told him to shut it and turned to focus on encouraging me to go for it. I swapped my left foot to my right to stretch out towards the arête of the wall. A chicken-head-shaped clump of rock was the hold I needed to get past and then the climb was mine. It was a grade 24, with the scale going from five to 32. I pulled myself onto the arête and balanced on the chicken head. The hardest part was over. The relief coursed through my body, making my blood feel warm. This memory reminded me that it was rare to be the author of your own fate. I had once held my life in my hands. The situation got reversed with cancer.

And what about those who don't survive? Are they losers? In *The Year of Magical Thinking*, American author Joan Didion explored the grief and shock to her psyche after her husband died from a massive heart attack, sitting upright at the dinner table. Her only daughter was dead within a year from septic shock after severe pneumonia. *If death catches you, you only have yourself to blame*, was Didion's suspicion of how others sometimes responded to her circumstance.

I found there was a kind of blame assigned to a person for developing cancer in the first place, as if there's a cancer type of person. Like you brought it on. Isn't that what I did when I said I wished my mother had chosen differently in her treatment – that she could have lived, but she died instead?

My death felt imminent. I didn't want to die young. I was 35. My mother developed breast cancer at 45 and died at 56, riddled with metastases from her womb to the lining of her skull. No thank you. It was scary and over-powering, as if a Greek god didn't like you. I wanted in on the survivors, on that group of people. I wanted to be someone who died of old age with a story to tell. But what about those among us who fight the disease and lose?

Beat and fight. Words that never sat well with my mother or me. She used the term *to dance with cancer* and that's what she did. Sometimes she stepped confidently without looking, as decisively as she would in an Argentinean tango: guided by the hand at her back. Other times she swayed on the spot with every beat causing goose pimples, summoning up the passion of a life lived in sound and fury: alive to the moment. She either leant into the movement of her dying swan or stamped angrily on her cancer partner's feet, hollering at its jerky rhythm and too-rapid pacing. At times she prayed the dance would never end.

I wouldn't dance with cancer. It was no friend of mine. I wasn't going to fight it either, declaring war on my own body.

I didn't like cancer, but my body had grown it. My body had once been good to me. It had *grand jeté*'d across stages, hauled me up cliff faces, held onto billowing spinnakers and trekked into high mountains. I wanted to work with my body to rid myself of it. Beating cancer made sense – I understood the term – I just didn't use it.

To fight cancer meant standing in a castle's turret volleying arrows down onto an attacking army as it tried to break down your reinforced healthy door – this wasn't the right image for the way it was treated. To *attack* cancer wasn't really the right medical term. To *suppress its chances of developing* was. With chemotherapy and hormone therapy I had suppressed the bejesus out of mine.

Breast reconstruction: what are the meanings of breasts?

... I was still feeling a strange stunned alertness, as if everything were taking place in slow motion, under halogen lights.

Brenda Walker, *Reading by Moonlight*

I arrived on time at my plastic surgeon's rooms. Pale velvety-cushioned chairs lined all three sides of the waiting room, with a low-lying table brimming with eye-catching magazines in the middle.

Celso wanted to practise his walking. He slapped his pudgy hands on the seats, one after the other, making his way along the perfect line of chairs. A kind woman opposite told me about her nine-month-old daughter who did the same. By this stage my boy was pulling all the neatly stacked magazines onto the floor, and then stomping on them. A fabulous poo stink reeked from his small person.

I'll need to find a spare room, I said to the front receptionist. She was stiff and starched. She rolled her eyes.

Inside the room I prepared the spongy black consultation bed as if I were about to perform an operation myself. Celso tried opening the chrome cupboards and bin so I clasped him between my knees before picking him up and laying him back on the black bed. I got out a biodegradable bag ready for the soiled nappy. I opened it up, un-stuck the frilly bit around the leg hole that stops stuff getting out, and pulled the first of his wipes out of their container. Because of Celso's reflux I placed his nappy bag under his head to elevate it. He squealed with displeasure.

It's okay, sweetie boo, I'm just making you more comfortable – promise! I said.

He tried rolling off the bed.

I grabbed his ankles to hold his bum off his soiled nappy before whipping it away into the orange bag.

Once cleaned he sat upright, turned onto his stomach and dangled his legs over the sides. I like your ambition, but it's not going to happen, I said, sitting him back up on his change quilt.

You cannot leave the dirty nappy in the bin, and you have to take it with you, I'd been told.

Yes, darling, I wanted to say. What else would I do with it? Eat it?

I knotted the stinky bag and dumped it into the pram's basket, planning to throw it into the first bin I saw outside on the street. I secured Celso back in his stroller and cleaned my hands.

Once inside, I faced my plastic surgeon, the man who was going to perform my breast reconstruction after a double mastectomy. Dr Theile was a dignified figure, too young for his light grey hair. He was reassuringly direct when I asked him about nipple-saving options. Well, if you're doing this to significantly reduce your risk of recurring breast cancer then why would you leave any breast tissue?

Good point.

I don't want to leave my nipples. I just wanted to ask about the difference, statistically, between nipple saving and removal. To know the chances of my surviving breast cancer, I said.

He put a rough figure together. It likely goes from 97 per cent to 90 per cent.

Can I look at some photos of reconstruction?

Sure.

He lit up his flat screen and an assortment of women's breasts appeared, their owners aged 29 to late 60s. The youngest woman had opted to forgo her nipple reconstruction and just use stick-on nipples, which worried Dr Theile as he hadn't finished his job for her.

An older woman's breast was reconstructed on one side using a TRAM flap procedure. A TRAM flap creates a new breast from abdominal fat, skin and muscle. The woman's other breast had to be lifted to match the newly bouncing bosom.

Celso reached across to grab a notepad. I pulled his hand back and jiggled him about on my knees. You can give him this, Dr Theile said, passing an unbreakable ampersand ornament.

Celso grabbed it and tried to fit it into his mouth. It wasn't a choke hazard so I let him and continued viewing the photos.

Another older woman had had a double mastectomy and immediate reconstruction. I saw her breasts in the inflation stage, where the flesh of the breasts was removed during a mastectomy and saline implants were inserted under the muscle on the chest wall – her chest held two child's balloons. It looked unnatural. Then I saw the result once the silicone implants were in after expanding the skin to the desired breast size. They looked pretty good. There were scars of course, long lines across the middle of the new breast, where a nipple used to be. The surgery and tattooing came later.

It would take four distinct steps to go from a double mastectomy to the finished result. My breast surgeon would remove the breast tissue, then the plastic surgeon would put in saline tissue expanders. When the scars healed enough I'd return to Dr Theile's rooms once a week for approximately ten weeks and he'd inject saline solution, through my skin, into the expanders, thereby stretching my skin and making my breast mounds bigger.

Once they inflated to the right size I'd go in and have the expanders removed and replaced with silicone implants. The surgical technique of a nipple tack, where they would cut and fold some skin from where the nipple had once been, would come after this, then areola tattooing once the 'nipples' healed.

Should I go with the size I am now? The thought went around as I looked at the other women's breasts.

At 34, in the early stages of pregnancy, I finally had a proper bra fitting at Myer and discovered that I wasn't a 12B after all, but a 10C. After Celso was born and I expressed for six months my breasts deflated. They were even smaller than they were pre-pregnancy. This was fine, but with the chance of a 'choose your own adventure' a robust 10C did sound nice.

Dr Theile remained calm with my squirming son and allowed him to sit on his desk as I asked questions. I'd given Celso an Old McDonald puppet book to play with, in which each finger had an animal to animate while singing. He was chomping down on the cardboard pages of the palm book and some of the paper had come away in his mouth. He choked on it straight away, so I flicked it out of his mouth and held a handkerchief up to his face, assuming he'd vomit. He didn't.

He okay? asked Dr Theile.

Celso resumed playing with the black and white cow on the puppet's thumb.

Yes, I replied.

Behind Dr Theile were framed pictures of his family. His good-looking wife once anchored the news in Brisbane and had her own professional standing in the community. In the photo she had her arms around their three children but still maintained the well-dressed-and-presentable-at-any-occasion appearance of a newsreader. The consultation room was large but seemed larger because the windows went from wall to wall and revealed a cityscape of office buildings.

Dr Theile's main concern with Celso sitting on his table was that he might fall off. Not that he might barf all over his private documents and silk tie. Big tick.

The first time I went to Dr Theile's rooms, B was in tow. Celso was cared for by a relative so we could focus in an adult way and spend time later talking through the decision in a café. It was four days after my diagnosis of breast cancer. In that first week B and I ran between doctors and decisions, trying to gain as much insight into the situation before saying yes or no to a lumpectomy or other medical interventions.

I saw pictures of women's breasts then too. I also stood in front of Dr Theile with my jeans undone and my top off so he could examine my caesar scar and stomach. After declaring, You don't have enough fat for a TRAM flap procedure, he got up and stood behind me, regarding my breasts in the mirror: Arms up. Okay. Arms down.

As I watched Dr Theile examine me I floated a little away from the situation. Here I was with two sets of male eyes staring intensely at my breasts. I wasn't sandwiched between two lusty but gentle Spanish beauties in some mega fantasy, but in a glowing white medical suite with a surgeon and my partner. It was as unsexy an experience as you could imagine.

Your breasts are small, he said.

And neat, thank you very much, I thought.

They haven't dropped, and they're firm. A good option would be silicone implants.

Err, thanks, I'll be on my way then.

You could go bigger if you wanted, he added.

They shrank a bit after Celso, I said.

Just that some women choose to change their shape if they're going with the silicone implant option.

I don't want Dolly Parton boobs, but I might go slightly larger – to fill out my bra more.

He smiled.

I shrugged. And that was that: new breasts were on the menu.

If I were a chimp I wouldn't have breasts unless I was lactating. We're the only mammals to grow breasts from puberty. I learnt from *Breasts: A Natural and Unnatural History* that the father of modern taxonomy, Carolus Linnaeus, named us mammals due to the female species having mammary glands. As Florence Williams wrote, *Breasts are us*.

I was still a relatively young woman, though the old automatic questions of *How do I look? Am I attractive?* were fading from importance in light of my diagnosis. Women can feel defined by how they present to men; in turn, how they present to themselves is defined by a man or by male desire.

I hoped to rid myself of that concern. If there was one internal assessor I didn't need, it was the ugly stick barometer.

Three weeks after I finished chemotherapy I walked back through the sliding doors of the day oncology unit. It can feel like a *most useless place. The Waiting Place*, as Dr Seuss said. There were four sections for different kinds of waiting – for different doctors and different types of treatment. I sat in the section for people waiting for their bloods to be taken, oncologist appointments and then chemotherapy sessions. We were a craggy, raddled bunch of women and men. I was the youngest. Again.

I handed a bag full of beautiful woollen balls to the ever-kind nurse at reception for volunteers to knit beanies, telling her, Here's a bag donated care of my mother. This reception nurse would die three years later from heart complications brought on by her diabetes. I'd grabbed the wool from a box labelled *Mum's Stuff* that morning. I'd been sorting and clearing. The boxes also held slides in pale cardboard cartons, each the size of an elegant cigarette packet from the 60s.

First year Humanities, Teaching: shape, function, feeling/form was written on one carton – from one of my mother's first lecturing positions. She'd taken photo montages of Liverpool (the port the *Titanic* set sail from) and a Free School (one of the radical movements in the 70s towards democratic education, where schools were run as a collective without a headmaster dictating terms). The montage was part of what I imagined as a course on Marxism and the class struggle: kids rough-housing, industrial buildings, slum-like working conditions, nice parks, municipal libraries, uniform backyards with clotheslines, perfect squares for growing your own vegetables behind ugly red brick terraces. Mum had educated herself out of her working-class upbringing. She'd escaped.

A plummy English voice always made her wince. It was more than just prejudice against the upper classes: it was political. As if she felt the hand of the British class system and her fate as an adopted Londoner like a hand on her head holding her down, squashing her ambition.

Among the academic slides there was a shot taken by my mother's adopted father, with whom she'd had an affinity. She was glum-faced, sitting in a striped deck chair, leaning away from her adoptive mother. Mum's black hair hid most of her beautiful face – she was all red lips, long legs and hidden eyes. Her family of three were on their only holiday in Italy together. Mum was 14 and would meet a boy who would write letters to her for a year.

I flicked through every one of the 200 slides for a glimpse of my mother's face, holding the miniature memory up to the light. I couldn't throw away any picture of her. I had to keep any memory, even if not my own.

In the waiting room, magazines dating from 2005 to near recent lay in wonky piles on coffee tables. There was always a disparity in the quality of reading materials at private and public hospitals. The TV was pumping out inane crud to a few watchers with dull eyes and their minds willingly turned off. I wanted the brighter places promised by Dr Seuss in *Oh, the Places You'll Go!* Where were the Boom Bands playing?

The powerful cancer-busting drugs bubbled and boiled a few metres from us. The chemist, who was shaped like a matryoshka doll, spoke to patients through her protective glass window. How can I help you, darling? She was efficient, with high energy.

I arrived that Friday at 8.15 a.m. and at 11 a.m. I saw my oncologist for a review. My portacath was accessed, bloods taken, urine sample provided and weight recorded. My temperature and pulse were taken (fine), and details of the most recent side effects duly noted (not great) by a pregnant research nurse from England. She was sensitive, with pale blue, almost white eyes that washed out – hid – her perceptiveness.

At that moment I was cancer free. I could say so without shuddering. I was freer than I'd been in months and calmed by the peekaboo dawn of good feeling. The gruelling chemo regimen was over. I wasn't sick. My mouth didn't provide a dash of metal with every meal like a sadistic saltshaker. I enjoyed food again. Hope had washed back in and surrounded my ankles. Cautious optimism stopped it from drowning me and blurring my vision. I was happier.

The next stop on the breast cancer train was breasts off.

It was 12 days into the new year and Kubrick's space odyssey still hadn't happened nine years after it should've. Humans were still grounded on Earth. Virgin could fly you through the stratosphere. If you could afford a sizeable house in Sydney's inner city you could float gravity free for a few minutes. But no, Earth was still our main residence. We paid an extra two dollars per plane ticket to minimise our carbon footprints in the sky, there was political argy-bargy on minimising emissions and many countries were experiencing extreme weather conditions – from snow covering all of England to catastrophic fires in Victoria, Australia.

I may have thought globally, but my world was still very much local. In a strange twist of fate, I visited the day oncology unit more often for my Zoladex injections now than I had for chemotherapy. I had Zoladex once a month, regular echocardiograms to check the drugs weren't compromising my heart muscle and IV Herceptin every three weeks to suppress the HER2 protein that my particular brand of breast cancer liked for breakfast.

Now that I was no longer undergoing chemotherapy and the intensive support had faded, I took Celso along for the ride. He attracted a lot of attention from the nurses. Fellow patients engaged with me in a way they wouldn't have if the subject hadn't been babies – mainly their own and their own's own. Celso was a bit of babbling sunshine and normality in a place where people were going through really difficult stuff and feeling sick along the way.

My new do in the new year was a faux Mohawk like David Beckham's, though greyer and thicker. Less than two months after my ovaries had been turned off, hot flushes were the worst of the menopausal symptoms. When the hot flushes came on it was like molten lava oozing out of a volcano. The heat was red hot, and consuming. My heart went from *thumpidy thump thump* to *boom boom* in an effort to manage whatever was happening internally with the rushes. I told a young nurse about this and she informed me that her aunt named them 'power surges'. They *were* powerful. Another nurse, an older one, provided some good advice:

Honey, mine used to help me get out of bed in the morning. I'd be all warm and tucked in, then the heat surge came on and I'd jump out of bed straight away. I knew I had ten minutes to get dressed without feeling the cold one little bit.

The hot flushes combined with the moist heat of the Brisbane summer made for many showers and changes of underwear.

I knew with the turn of this year my mastectomy surgery was impending.

But how do you prepare for a mastectomy?

You can't.

Part of what killed my mother was her need to be feminine. She baulked at full removal when first diagnosed with cancer and only allowed the surgery after her third occurrence. It'll affect my notion of myself as a woman, she'd said when we first discussed a mastectomy.

I wrote an ode on my blog to my mammaries by way of saying goodbye:

If there's a mammary heaven mine will be with friends soon.
The message I want them to take to mammary paradise is not
to be good girls, but saucy minxes. May they flirt with anyone
that flies by; may they bare all without shame; may they flop
down in some angel's lap and cause them to blush.
Dear mammaries, how I'll miss you.

I'd loved my 'ladies', but I'd never had the sensual connection that some women talked of. I enjoyed them. I liked their shape. I was glad, though, that the intense bind of femininity to breast wasn't present in me.

The last day of my original body was 31 January 2010. On 1 February I would become a cyborg. Living was wilder than any story I could imagine. Emotional preparation aside, I clicked into *doing* mode: *getting rid of cancer* mode.

My first female anaesthetist did a stellar job. She phoned me the Friday before mastectomy Monday and talked through my prior bad anaesthetic reactions and how she was going to handle things. I took two Phenergan (anti-histamine, anti-nausea) pills at 11 a.m., and by 1.30, when I was due to go into theatre, I could barely remain awake, slumped over the side of the well-padded chairs, drooling.

When the time came to go in, my breast surgeon loomed over me to confirm I knew exactly what was about to happen. He had a blue tinge under each eye, as if he'd been working too hard or too late. Okay? he asked.

I'm in the middle of one of the weirdest days of my life.

He gripped my left shoulder in sympathy, and then I was wheeled into theatre.

And.

Action.

In my case the procedure was this: my breast surgeon made a circular incision around my nipple, taking it away, and then through the opening removed all the breast tissue. In some women breast tissue can go up under the armpit, which mine did, so the surgeon travelled up there through the same incision site. This part of the operation took two hours. He had to scrape the underside of my skin to remove every bit of breast tissue attached there.

Next Dr Theile entered the theatre and performed the last stage – the reconstruction. He inserted saline tissue expanders into both breasts through the same open site, and then sewed me up. I would have one long scar across each breast, with no nipple. It would resemble more of a boy's chest than a woman's until the expanders started to stretch my skin out. Dr Theile inserted drains through small cuts he made on the side of my torso into the breast mound area and sutured them in place. The drains usually stayed in for one week. This part of the operation took another two hours. All up, I was under a general anaesthetic for four-and-a-bit hours.

When I first woke up after surgery I kept saying, I feel weird, I feel weird, to a newly minted nurse from Queensland University of Technology. I didn't need to ask what her role was; it was embroidered on her blue-collared QUT shirt. She was pumping up the blood pressure cuff. An IV line was delivering fluids on the same side as the blood pressure cuff and it hurt like hell.

B was beside me. He sat next to me reading for several hours until I woke up. In times like these B was my knight, standing guard to make sure I was treated well and everything was okay medically. He translated my discomfort for the nurse. I was protected.

Back into the sleep abyss. No dreaming.

Awoken again.

I need to go back. Sophie's looking after Celso, he said. Sophie was B's lovely cousin.

Okay pea, you go. I slipped back into the dark.

I finally came round at midnight saying the same thing: I feel weird. This time there had been a shift change and the night staff were older sisters, stern but capable. I longed for their hand or ear. They came and went.

The first time I stood my jaw quivered; my whole body quaked.

This is normal, just post-op shock and the anaesthetic wearing off, said the formidable nurse. The back of her head was flat, but her face was strong.

I didn't sleep the first night without my breasts. I had come to dread being awake in a hospital, tied to the bed with tubes and catheters. This night alone with my thoughts was no different, like my time post–Celso's birth, but I had no nausea so I was okay. I loved my anaesthetist. Without her preparatory phone call I wouldn't have coped so well.

If my mother had undergone a double mastectomy in 1996 she likely would have lived. Fourteen years later, I sat upright in bed with two drains taking the excess blood away from my wounds. A TV was high up on the other side of the wall. On my left a large sliding glass door framed a city view with glimpses of the Brisbane River. The decision was mine, all mine. But if it wasn't for my mother's decisions and breast cancer experience I wouldn't have been in that hospital bed. My mother's death, I realised, saved my life.

Have you opened your bowels? asked the same nurse from the day before, who'd hurt my arm taking my blood pressure.

No, not yet.

Are you getting wind or rumbling in your stomach? she added.

Yes.

Okay, well, walk around again today and drink plenty of water.

Done deal.

Four hours under anaesthetic slows down the body. It's like putting a frog in a fridge. My lymphatic system – which transports excess protein and waste product from blood and tissues – was sluggish. I had puffy hands. The physiotherapist came around on day one to put me through my paces.

When I was able to walk without aid I took myself off to get a magazine on the ground floor as the physio suggested. I wore B's pyjama top (blue with red polo players), pink monkey pyjama bottoms, my leg-constricting leggings, ankle socks, Bonds sticky slippers, and no chest. I wondered if people thought I was a 'he'. At the elevator a woman mistook me for a visitor, asking, Who are you here to see? She was one democratic thinker.

Despite everything I still felt the same sense of relief I'd first woken with, without my breasts. I was literally and figuratively lighter. This feeling never wavered. There is nothing like death staring into your eyes for mental toughness. But my nightlife took on other emotions. It was as if a large whiteboard recorded my nightmarish dreams and in the morning I'd reach for the duster and quickly wipe the words and images away. Some were drawn with black marker and were hard to remove; faint traces remained until the following night, when another hallucinatory dream wrote over and changed the previous day's faded nightmares.

In one of them I was empathising with another young woman whose mother had died and I said, I remember the second time my mother died. We were in some hospital ward with old medical machinery around. Then I was inside a hospice – one without dignity – and watched my mother wake up from being dead. She'd come back to life. It was real and made sense in my dream and also when I woke. My experience of going through cancer treatment after caring for my mother as she went through hers made me relive her death and everything that had led up to it. My mother had died twice. The first time hadn't counted. I understood her death more now, as I had come close to mine.

It was as if I had a door marked *breast cancer*. Once I opened it, it drew in others who had also experienced the disease. A big, kind woman who served the hospital meals had had breast cancer two years prior to my diagnosis, but she'd been clear ever since. She told me this after she'd enquired about my chest bandaging. She said she took her hormonal medication every other day because it played havoc with her. I would be too frightened to do this, equating this decision to taking the contraceptive pill every other day: you'd risk getting something you didn't want.

On day three the nurse came to sponge bath me. It was my first look at my body, albeit with dressings on, in the mirror. The constricting bandages gave me a cliff of a chest.

Part of protecting your lymphatic system against lymphedema is to maintain well-moisturised skin. After enlivening mine I did the *does my bum look big in this* side to side, glancing in the bathroom mirror. I was 163 centimetres tall and weighed 52 kilograms, and my hair was short and thick-wavy like Mia Farrow's in her Sinatra days. I might've been 35, but the image before me was of a tall 11-year-old boy. I was pre-adolescent again. Flat on the back and front. My shoulders were broad; when I was a girl, T-shirts used to hang down before breasts interrupted the curtain look and made a woman out of me. The renewed flat-chestedness was familiar. I'd lived through the emergence of womanly bits before. I was a changeling. Though this time my form would be female but my fertility would not.

When my plastic surgeon took my dressing off, I glimpsed my chest, but I wasn't prepared for a full-frontal investigation. I remembered too well my mother's left breastplate after her mastectomy: concave with an angry red-purple dash across it like the Joker's smile. I didn't want to see mine. On the other hand the pain was less than I imagined and I only required Panadol for a week to control the discomfort.

I had my breasts removed around the time of Mum's birthday. It was a strange day. I sat up in my hospital bed knowing that what killed her was hopefully behind me. I'd written to the surgeon who'd performed her mastectomy, asking for the details of her treatment as he knew it. I received the answer on what would've been her 61st birthday. It told me of the decisions I knew about, like no to chemotherapy, no to radiation, yes … eventually, to mastectomy and close monitoring. The dates were the important part for me. Like some kind of medical bookkeeper I wanted to match up my recall of events with dates and my mother's progression towards the grim reaper.

The terms and medical reality of breast cancer were part of my language now. But at 22, when I'd held my mother's hand, reassuring her that the lumpectomy scar wasn't that bad, I was sure her fate wasn't my own. Wrong.

I found myself leaping back and forth between her experience and my own. For breakfast in hospital I'd ritually open the lid of my morning prunes and dump them in my rolled oats. Of course this meal assisted the 'opening of my bowels', something that became quite dire for Mum.

A thought shot over the bow of time to what I saw of her life during breast cancer. A ray of guilt zapped me when one day in the last fortnight of my mother's life I walked into her hospital room and found her asleep with her meal untouched in front of her. No nurse had attempted to assist her to eat. Even in my mother's awake, semi-conscious state, she couldn't pick the spoon up and bring it to her mouth. I did this for her.

Tess (my aunt-in-kind) raised her camera to take a photograph in the last week when Mum would only take food if I fed it to her. I stopped her, knowing Mum wouldn't have liked an eternal recording of the indignity of the situation.

I left hospital after four days. Two weeks after the procedure I saw my plastic surgeon. My chest area was hypersensitive; it was a strange, disembodied feeling. I explained the sensation to Dr Theile:

Imagine wearing a fat suit over your body after a severe car accident left you bruised and lacerated.

He was above me, staring down with clasped hands and a focussed but bemused expression. I was topless on his examination table. I lifted my head to peer at my chest. I was a flat plain. No breast mounds obscured my view of my stomach. I was more adolescent male than female with defined stomach muscles and broad shoulders, apart from the red, healing cuts. Like this, I could get away with wearing swimming trunks only on the beach. If I touched near the incision points my un-inflated saline implants crinkled like cellophane.

I continued my disembodied story to Dr Theile. An old friend comes to wish you luck and pats you on your fat suit – because you look funny – right over the area where your ribs connected with the steering wheel.

Dr Theile grimaced and swayed. The fluorescent light behind him made me squint.

You see him touch the fat suit, but can't feel the contact. What you feel is the pressure of his finger directly over the wounded area. The disconnect between sensations is deeply disturbing.

Dr Theile then touched my chest and I almost jumped off the examination table.

I'll start inflating you in one week, he said, snapping off his gloves.

Three weeks after my mastectomy I was back in the examination room, topless again. Dr Theile had a nurse who was also his secretary perform the saline injections into the tissue expander if he was busy. On my expander was a valve shaped like a pincushion, the size of a 50-cent piece. Inside it was a magnet. She put a divining gadget the size of a mobile phone over my breast mounds to align magnet to magnet. I saw worry in her widened eyes. I haven't done this before, she said.

I became frightened and focussed on steadying my breathing. I knew that if she missed, a shooting pain would go up into my armpit. She found the magnets and inserted a needle through the skin and muscle into the valve. Clunk. She'd missed. Pain shot into my right armpit. She got it second go. Sixty millilitres would be injected into each expander every week until I was the desired size.

Medical anthropologist Professor Lenore Manderson has written about people's experiences of their bodies after catastrophic change. I loved how she examined the ways people re-made themselves. I too was establishing a different sense of my own body and self. The sickness that permeated everything during chemotherapy had predominantly lifted. In the many surgeries, and my status as someone whose life was threatened, I found a radicalising principle.

Just as my forced menopause springboarded me into considering older women in society and how they felt about socially desired bodies, breast removal realigned my view of my own femininity. As a changeling going through a kind of puberty again, I was aware that part of the social construction of femininity is around women's breasts: having them, showing them, milking them. Yet I now chose exactly what size and shape of breast I had and showed to society. They didn't require a bra and would appear *perfect* in clothes until I died and they were cremated alongside the flesh I was born with. (It's not necessarily a one-off operation. Silicone implants do need checking to see if replacement is required from rupture, capsular contracture or scar tissue. Every ten years I'll return to my plastic surgeon to have them checked.) When I caught a man's lingering look, I smiled to myself with the thought, *I'm fooling you, aren't I?*

The ever-present scarring across my chest stood for the disease and the surgery. Manderson researched many women's responses to their post-surgical bodies. In her findings the scar also represented the breast, femininity and sexuality. My scars didn't bother me, psychically, like they did my mother. She once asked, Don't you mind me like this? Referring to her bald head from chemotherapy and her one-breasted chest.

Mum, I couldn't care less what your appearance is. You're beautiful and I love you. Your lack of hair and one breast mean absolutely nothing to me, I replied.

And it appeared that, for B, the same was true. At night, with our son asleep, he turned to me – with my bald head, half breasts and emaciated body.

Cancer etiquette:
does cancer change you?

*But the cloud never comes in that quarter of the horizon
from which we watch for it.*

Elizabeth Gaskell, *North and South*

It was 5.40 a.m. the day after my 36th birthday, and I was on
my way to Mater Private. Floor lights were on in the office
buildings. There was little activity in the street. Dawn was an
hour away. It could have been any time of night.

We make so many laws we become lawless, said the
tattooed, middle-aged taxi driver. A man the other day got
unintentional death for killing a man at a taxi rank. He thought
a guy pushed in so he king-hit him. At first it was murder,
then manslaughter, then unintentional death and now off on
a good behaviour bond. A man can divorce a woman over the
internet and she's left without a leg to stand on … Sometimes
I want to divorce the world, he concluded.

Okay, thanks, I said and shut the taxi door.

In front of me were the sliding doors to the entrance. The day
had come. My new breasts lay somewhere within this building.

When I was suited up in the familiar truckers' undies,

stockings, back-to-front dress and flannel dressing gown I sat down in the plush area for patients awaiting procedures. The noise of the TV intruded into the silence: there was news of a nurse whose throat was cut by a former patient. I jerked as if slapped. I tried to calm myself down by focussing on the exhalation through my nose. I took two Phenergan to relax me, which I now knew assisted the post-anaesthesia nausea. By the time I was on the trolley ready to go in I was tranquillised cool.

What are you having done? the anaesthetic technician asked. Everyone, from admitting nurses to surgeons, had to check I knew what was about to happen.

Changing my saline inserts for silicone ones – new boobs today. I smiled up at him with a goofy *I've taken drugs* expression. My breast expanders acted like a water-bed and the pitter-pat rhythm of my heart sent waves through the saline solution. I watched my heart beating its watery song for a second.

The technician had the well-rounded vowels of a good education, and a light touch. He joked and was sensitive to my situation; I was a woman about to have breast surgery for the third time. Once I was under the bright alien lights of the operating theatre he busied himself attaching my scuds (leg pumps), arranging me and teaching a trainee technician.

The trainee put sticky monitors on my back and went to put a blood pressure cuff on my right arm – the arm that had had nine lymph nodes removed from its armpit. After a sentinel node biopsy the arm cannot be used to take blood pressure, as a precaution against lymphedema.

Not there, on the calf, said my anaesthetist. He was slapping a vein on the back of my left hand to get an access point. It hurt.

The trainee didn't understand him properly.

Her calf! Do you know what a calf is?

The main technician jumped in and showed his underling the ropes. I saw the shame and suppressed annoyance in the trainee's eyes. The man appeared of Sri Lankan or Indian origin. I felt for him. He had a lovely, humane smile.

I found out after this operation that once you're under a general they often put tape over your eyes. I roused from the general with purple shading under both of mine from an allergic reaction to the tape. The head nurse told me that they tape eyelids if they are flickering or remain open(ish).

I summoned the image of standing next to a person you were about to operate on. I would find the flickering-eye thing distracting too. After they've taped your eyelids shut, they intubate you – insert a tube into your throat to take over your breathing. The thought always made me breathe in deeply like my throat was constricting.

The comfort of two orbs on my chest went right into my skull. My sense of myself as still female, due to my false breasts' very existence, did the trick. The red dashes marked where my nipples once were.

The pain post-surgery was minimal. An oddity of my new false breasts was that I could make them go up and down. I figured if muscle was used to secure my silicone implants then I should be able to flex my pecs. Once after a shower I stood in front of the mirror and flexed one then the other: *rat ta tat tat.* They looked like breasts but beneath I was She Robot.

The traumas of my 30s dissolved my selfhood until 'I' became a quilt pieced together by traumatic experiences, memories and various educations. If someone had asked me to describe what I did or who I was I'd have to wrap the quilted self around my shoulders and read off the patches. Well, I did this two years ago, and that seven years ago … so I guess I'm a …

There'd been an accumulation of depersonalising experiences: my body changing under the knife and facing cancer, and what that meant for my living a possibly shortened life. What I'd planned was no longer going to happen; what lay ahead was most definitely unknown. What was in front of me was, was … what? At this point I was blinking in the new dawn of being cancer free. I had a changeling body, from adolescent to woman, but also a changeling mind. My identity appeared fluid.

Hair gave character; you changed it and people drew different conclusions about you. My long locks feminised me. I had done a lot of dancing and outdoor adventuring in my life and my arm muscles (from climbing) were prominent. I used to feel my body had a natural tendency towards the masculine. This belief was inflated by my diagnosis of polycystic ovaries, but my long, feminine locks counteracted the perception I had of myself.

Before chemotherapy started I got a short do and loved the younger-looking self in the mirror. When I went bald I joined the cancer community and became one of them. With no hair on my head, up my nose, and little left on my eyebrows and eyelashes, I was desexualised.

When the spiky beginnings of my hair appeared after chemotherapy, I noticed a change in how people saw me. We'd had our first fun time together as a family on the victory holiday in New Zealand.

We'd driven a Happy Camper, their basic model with a small kitchenette and seats that converted to bedding. We hung

Celso's feeding formula bag off a hook, which we set up on a window latch.

My son has Down syndrome, the woman had told us on our arrival at the oversize luggage area to collect the backpack with Celso's formula bags. She was in her 50s with faded blonde hair and an open face. I think it's great you continuing to travel as a family, she said, that's important. She waved us off with a broad smile.

We'd packed enough formula to last a fortnight, with extras in case something happened, plus an extra kangaroo feeding pump. This pump was kept charging off the camper's engine battery, while the other was in use. Australia has a reciprocal health care agreement with New Zealand so we knew if Celso became ill or his peg got pulled out we could rush to a nearby hospital.

Celso had had a peg put in as his not eating appeared semi-permanent. The temporary nasogastric tube we'd been using to keep him alive, hoping he'd pick up eating and drinking, was no longer viable. He pulled it out too often and, really, enough was enough for him after having it taped to his face for the first 18 months of his life. It was unlikely to come out but it had happened once, soon after the peg had been inserted. We'd gone for a day out to the Botanic Gardens, as he loved the ponds with their large goldfish. When I put him back into his front-facing car seat, the temporary thick tube, which stays in until the site heals and toughens into a large version of an ear piercing, got stuck on the seat belt unbeknownst to me. I put him in, feeling some resistance but thinking it was just clothing tucked in somewhere. The tube ripped out, his stomach contents immediately oozing out of the hole.

Sick and appalled at what I'd done, I shoved two nappies over the site to absorb and slow down the seeping formula and rushed to the Children's Hospital. It's okay, darling, I yammered at Celso over my shoulder. It's okay. I'm so sorry, honey. Mummy didn't know it was stuck in the seat belt. We'll get it fixed now. Don't worry.

They got us straight into the triage nurse's observation room and she put it back in. The skin hadn't ripped, nor had the newly made surgical hole closed up. Throughout the hours waiting in the hospital to see if the new insert took, Celso looked around and made use of the room around him to have fun. He does this. He examined the baby weigher with its scooped sides, placing his weight on it to see the numbers changing, and giggled; he *read* the glary pictures of giraffes and birds on the walls around him for meaning.

In the New Zealand airport, I stood in the duty-free line with a packet of cigars for a family member. A burly man with a shaved head behind the counter said, I love your haircut, it's great seeing women with short hair. I blanched, amazed that anyone found my buzz cut appealing. I explained in a hurried fashion that the decision for short hair wasn't really mine and that, no, I didn't get cancer from smoking, despite the cigars in my hand.

In the same period of regrowing my hair I took my son into the wading pool at our local swimming centre. Somewhere under 50 kilos, I still had my muscular appearance; in fact the chemo body-stripping had emphasised my musculature. I wore a bikini with a white singlet over it and as I was lifting and bouncing Celso in the water my biceps resembled a triathlete's. I faked fit well. A lesbian couple with their daughter kindly

118

approached me in the pool to make conversation, because I was clearly without a partner that day while everyone else had their families around them. One of the women, tall and built like a basketball player, introduced her partner and child to my son and me. We talked kiddie talk as all parents do and I could tell that they thought I was a lesbian too. This time I wasn't a member of the cancer community. I was in the lesbian one. The conversation was pleasant and we each said a warm See you next time.

My buzz cut received second glances in the Blue Room cinema, in an affluent suburb of Brisbane, but familiar greetings in alternative cafés.

Six months on from the mastectomy I was part of a media awareness campaign on breast cancer and, I realised, the feminising of oneself again. The very thing I thought I'd escaped the desire for.

Through the Choices support program, hair care manufacturer Nak provided three women with free natural hair extensions, hair dye and cuts for a year. The *Today* morning show on Channel 9 ran a three-minute interview with us about the impact of losing hair from breast cancer treatment. The segment was called 'Hair Hope'. I walked out that day with a Kristen Stewart version of Joan Jett on my head. Robin Bailey, a radio personality, did before and after interviews for Think Pink Week, which raised money for the Choices program. Once the hair extensions came out I had a Japanese anime femme fatale look: ragged, short fringe, and straight, dragged-through-a-hedge-backwards sides. My hair gave off an edge of cool I didn't feel.

People responded to how I looked post-cancer. They also responded to the fact of my cancer. It appeared that both of these things unearthed deep fears of their own death. I was drawn to Joan Didion's reflections on this phenomenon in *The Year of Magical Thinking.* She wrote:

We are imperfect mortal beings, aware of that mortality even as we push it away, failed by our very complication, so wired that when we mourn our losses we also mourn, for better or for worse, ourselves. As we were. As we are no longer. As we will one day not be at all.

How people reacted to my cancer news has made me think there is a need for cancer etiquette now that so many people are diagnosed with it. That people should be careful what they say. Like when you're pregnant: for some reason the bump opens up the Pandora's box of hellish birth stories that passing acquaintances must tell you about. Ditto cancer.

One day at Celso's playgroup I stood watching him playing around a tunnel in a jungle gym. He was contemplating going through it – head in, then out, squirm halfway in, then squirm out. The week before I'd made a pitch for The Ride to Conquer Cancer: a 200-kilometre ride over two days to raise funds for the QIMR Berghofer Medical Research Institute. My team, Breast Friends for a Cure, were raising funds. After announcing this, of course, I was the go-to person to discuss cancer with. This was fine by me. Though on this day I was left smiling with amusement from the sheer verbal battering.

You had breast cancer? a mother asked.

Yes.

Did you have a mastectomy?

Yes, both breasts, I replied, pointing to my reconstructed breasts.

I got a text this morning that my friend's wife died last night from breast cancer.

Oh, I'm so sorry to hear that.

She was young like you. It was aggressive and she died really quickly.

Words jangled in my mouth but I didn't spit any out. Hmm ... I kept my eyes straight ahead on Celso at the top of the slide, now in full sun.

On my way out of the playgroup a volunteer assistant stopped me to ask if I'd seen the show on TV the night before about a mother's breast cancer experience.

I was about to tell him I didn't have a TV in my living room, but instead said, No, I didn't.

I heard it was really good. It was called 'My Breasts Could Kill Me'.

By this stage I wanted to raise my hands in the air, look up to the sky and yell, Listen to what you are saying, people.

In the same week I was bombarded at playgroup, a close family friend tried to reassure me: Celso would be taken care of if God forbid you weren't around.

I wished to face my own mortality alone, without others openly addressing their passing thoughts on my death. The late writer Christopher Hitchens in his regular *Vanity Fair* column expressed similar confrontations. One in particular made me in turn laugh then grimace.

An elderly woman approaches him at a book signing and relays how her cousin had liver cancer, which went away then returned more aggressively. Christopher Hitchens does his public-school English cough and turns on his charming self to offer his condolences.

She fails to feel the many eyes on her head wishing her to move away and relays how her cousin died alone and in agony – oh, and that he was a homosexual his whole life. She concludes with the unthoughtful words of, I know exactly how you feel, which of course she never could.

In Hitchens's piece he makes the argument that ground rules for interactions between people from Tumortown and Wellville are needed, especially as more and more people are inhabiting *that other place*.

Joan Didion turned to Emily Post's seminal book on etiquette for advice around grief and how people ought to respond to the grief-stricken:

Persons under the shock of genuine affliction are not only upset mentally but are all unbalanced physically. No matter how calm and controlled they seemingly may be, no one can under such circumstances be normal. Their disturbed circulation makes them cold, their distress makes them unstrung, sleepless. Persons they normally like, they often turn from. No one should ever be forced upon those in grief, and all over-emotional people, no matter how near or dear, should be barred absolutely. Although the knowledge that their friends love them and sorrow for them is a great solace, the nearest afflicted must be protected from any one or anything which is likely to overstrain nerves already at the threatening point, and none have the right to feel hurt if they are told they can neither be of use or be received. At such a time, to some people companionship is a comfort, others shrink from their dearest friends.

So too a cancer diagnosis and living with the disease. My immediate thought was *So this is how I'm going to die.*

I'd both lived as a person with cancer and experienced an intense grieving period. For six months after my mother's death I did not work, I did not watch TV, I did not drink alcohol and I didn't want to discuss my grief, as it was mainly inarticulate. I exiled myself and gave way to 'sitting' with my loss. If I were of a tradition that wore a black band on my arm to indicate mourning I would have done so. Alma Whittaker in Elizabeth Gilbert's grand novel *The Signature of All Things* expressed it perfectly when she said: *There is a level of grief so deep that it stops resembling grief at all. The pain becomes so severe that the body no longer feels it. The grief cauterizes itself, scars over, prevents inflated feelings. Such numbness is a kind of mercy.*

To live with cancer was to grieve one's former life, even when in remission. So too to witness a loved one die from the disease. Cancer scares people to the quick. It was not surprising that people gave inappropriate advice about alternative treatments. Though one person blamed my disease on my mental state, everyone else, medical staff and close friends and family, was truly sympathetic. It was just their tongues' expressions of sympathy that sometimes got tied.

Mothering and cancer:
is motherhood ever enough?

But it is a hallmark of the damaged that when it comes to their own desire instinctively, ruinously, they tend to court its opposite.

Salley Vickers, *The Other Side of You*

My mother was a 'bastard' child, conceived at the beginning of the Cold War in 1948. Her mother was a Welsh woman in her 20s studying stage design, and her father an Englishman named 'Jim'.

A London working-class couple adopted my mother: Heather Mary Dietrich. Well, if she can't walk then she'll really need loving parents. Won't she? said my mother's adopted father. This was the folk tale told to me over the years.

My mother was born with a prominent bump at the base of her spine. The medical staff on the London maternity ward imprisoned her biological mother on the ward to comb old people's hair. She had to stay around and make herself useful in case her baby was disabled and unplaceable. Mum ended up with one leg longer than the other. Her out-of-kilter hips caused her back to kink and required a chiropractor to clunk her spine into line. Later on I'd need the same.

My mother's beginning would affect her entire emotional make-up. It was a branding for her: abandonment. Her sense of rejection at birth skewed her view when choosing partners. I once joked that she could walk into a room and pick the worst man for her in seconds. She laughed, because it was true.

When Mum reached her 20s she tracked down her biological mother and they finally met face to face in an English pub. My mother had ducked her head under the thick beam of a centuries-old pub and scanned the room. Through the cymbal and crash of drinks being served and noisy banter she'd spotted the only person who could be a relation. A woman with grey hair, soft skin and cautious blue eyes: her mother. The real one. The content of the conversation was a fast-paced summing-up of facts: this school, this course, this house. She left fantasising about what her life would have been if that mother had mothered her. To have had a connection of the mind growing up. She'd loved speaking with an educated and interesting mother, not one at odds to her. When she tried to discuss her biological mother, her adopted mother would collapse down the living-room wall, wailing. When she wasn't a good girl her adopted mother would caution, We didn't have to have you, you know.

You couldn't breed out the Welsh retroussé nose. My grandmother's nose was my mother's, mine and my son's. All of my mother's Welsh line resided in Wales.

In light of the tendency towards breast cancer in my immediate family, my biological grandmother's cancer-less status intrigued me. She'd undergone a radical hysterectomy after the birth of her last child, which might have saved her due to the oestrogen drop. Or, the tendency towards cancer was inherited from the unknown father, my maternal grandfather. Who knew?

Mum and I had many conversations about her being a grandmother and me a mother when I was 'older'. You'll marry, have two-point-five children and a Labrador, she'd say. I'd giggle, lower my eyes and a bubble would form above my head, with the image of a happy marriage that was mine. I did want this, and if I stood in the present and glanced around at my unwedded marriage I had the happy union of my imaginings.

Mum had a counsellor's ability to listen, really listen to you, matched with a reverence for people and the human predicament. She went to the depth of the thing that you wanted to discuss, or she could spend hours on an intellectual conundrum. I felt valued and *seen* by my mother, who was my confidant and a soul-mate for 31 years.

What terrified me the most about my mother dying was that I might not be able to survive without her. I'd be marooned with all my blood-relatives half a world away. Abandoned in the adopted country. It didn't matter that I was 31. These digits could easily have been reversed.

Mum and I would mooch in a café, drinking tea and conjuring up what kind of life I might lead as a mother. What would I do? What would my partner look like? There was always uneasiness when I imagined giving birth. When I was 17 and we lived in Canberra (Mum had to move there for a full-time job in government) I was diagnosed with polycystic ovarian syndrome (PCOS). My menstrual cycle had staggered into a half-life when I was 14, and though at the time we figured the low fat content of my ballet and gym body was the cause, it wasn't.

PCOS is a shitty thing for a woman to have. Think of it as a spectrum disorder with the left side being manageable but the extreme end on the right being downright nasty. In brief, my ovaries were sensitive and overly stimulated. They produced excessive amounts of androgens through the release of too much luteinising hormone (LH) or insulin in the blood. In the menstrual cycle your LH does her thing, preparing the ovarian follicles to grow big enough for an egg to pop into them. The follicle later bursts and the egg goes down the fallopian tube. However, if the follicle-stimulating hormone (FSH) sheila at this critical egg-popping point gets all shy and doesn't yell out loud enough for the LH to hear her shouting the words, Work with me over here, then your eggs don't ripen.

What? says LH. I can't hear you.

The sad thing was that my LH and FSH didn't work well together. In some women LH has a hearing aid and gets what FSH wants and makes contact; in others they never connect. If your LH and FSH never speak to one another then you remain infertile.

At 17 PCOS scared the hell out of me. I did two things with the verdict: ignored its existence, and silently feared like hell that hair would spring up in unwomanly places on my body. I was on the left-hand side of the spectrum and didn't suffer terribly with PCOS, but if you were on the extreme end you were obese, suffered from acne and hirsutism, with diabetes thrown into the mix, and you were likely infertile.

Basically it was anti-beauty material, everything a developing girl would not want. It permanently fixed in me the idea that I wasn't normal like other girls.

As an adolescent I had the vanity of Narcissus. PCOS didn't do much for my entry into female adulthood. It destroyed the joy of a developing body in some ways, though in others not so – like my first sexual experience, which was easy, filled with lust (midnight cycles across town) and liberation. Despite that, because of PCOS traits I assumed I was somehow more masculine.

What really worried me was the infertility question. I figured nature's joke would be that I'd have to adopt, after having a mother who was adopted, and it would be some sort of *learn this lesson* life experience for both of us.

My mother told me many times the story of my drug-free birth. A 24-hour labour of agony, which split my mother right down to her perineum thanks to forceps. I was also a month overdue. I'd been due on 1 April.

My narrow hips made me think I'd suffer a screamer of a labour like my mother. Plus, I could never imagine giving birth. I know, I know … no woman can until she's in the throes of it. But in my life I've had visions of things I could do, a sense of my capacity, and I could never see myself giving birth. When I did have daydreams about it something dramatic would happen, like I'd haemorrhage afterwards (as I ended up doing) and appear to be dying, as in an Irish drama piece about a good Catholic girl giving birth in a cow shed on piles of hay. My husband would wipe his bloody hands on his work pants and lean his dark, curling head close to mine, crying, Don't leave me, I love you so.

I also had waking dreams about my future 'husband'. He'd appeared to me with a scarred face. B was in a serious car accident as an 18-year-old and sports a Harry Potter gash across his forehead. Maybe I did get these visions right?

As I was rendered menopausal by hormonal treatment, the issue of my PCOS seemed to have disappeared. Result. I didn't have to worry about hormonal imbalances of high oestrogen and progesterone; my chemical romance had put paid to these. I only had to wax body hair from my armpits or my legs every few months. Thanks to plastic surgery, I had the exact breasts of my choosing and I didn't have to wear a bra under dresses or backless tops. Plus, I would never pancake. How good was this for a 36-year-old mother?

When my mother's body was killing her, our roles reversed. I was mother to my mother. When I walked behind her flower-strewn coffin with a native Australian bouquet in my arms, tears streaming down my face and my chest heaving, I was her daughter again. Four years after her death when I was thrown by my own breast cancer diagnosis, I had Celso.

I bargained with some external power that I would be satisfied if I had the gift of life fully return after cancer treatment and that my reparation for that gift would be unfailing, uncomplaining motherhood. Prior to the diagnosis I'd taken it for granted that mothering a baby would be an intense phase of my adult life, and a situation that would 'get better' and change as my baby grew. I would go on, happily, to do other meaningful things with my life. But after diagnosis all I wanted was the motherhood role.

At times, before cancer, I wanted to straighten my feminist spine and roar: Let women stay at home with their children until school age if they please. As one highly intelligent and successful friend asked, But what do you say at parties when people ask, What do you do?

Where did feminism go wrong?

When my friend posed that question, Celso was six months old and still nasogastrically fed, refused to eat or drink, and frequently vomited day and night. He also required physiotherapy, occupational therapy, speech therapy and close monitoring by specialist doctors. So my answer to the question would've been: I'm a full-time mother. And sometimes: I'm a full-time mother of a high-needs baby.

To break down my response more fully I would have to say: One, I don't go to parties. Two, when did we cancel out mothering like it doesn't count? And if mothering doesn't count then my answer to What do you do? would be, Nothing: right now I'm just a mother at home. On your curriculum vitae there are no spaces for how many children you've cared for or parents you've nursed. That space is left blank. The years of lost employment.

I wanted acknowledgement of a hard job done with love and no pay. But the irony was that, after breast cancer, stay-at-home mothering wasn't enough for me either. I was as *bad* as my friend's question.

Helen Hayward, author of *A Slow Childhood*, sidelined a successful career to care for her children until she was in her 50s. She nailed the feeling for me in an essay, 'My Children, My Life':

What credits my sisters and me in the eyes of the world, and to some extent our own, is the work we do on top of the families we raise. Every day, I pour as many hours into my family and housekeeping than into my writing and editing, yet I'm recognised only for what I do beyond the home ... My children give me enormous pleasure and pride, a love so profound it escapes words. But my sense of identity and worth, and my inner buoyancy, stem from my work beyond them ... We're not content simply to put our children to bed at the end of the day and put our feet up until morning. We refuse to accept that love and ambition don't go together: we'd sooner toe the party line that career and family are happy bedfellows than accept the awkward truth of how hard that is. Even if the price is to be forever on the go. Yes, we've sacrificed our free time. But at least, we tell ourselves, we haven't sacrificed ourselves.

It was winter in Brisbane. The weather was perfect. It was possible to garden at noon without a hat, for instance. I pulled down the winter box of clothing from atop our old three-door dresser. I took out the clothes I wanted for the coming cooler months, and folded and packed my summer dresses and tops. I put away a few of Mum's remaining clothes, clothes she made herself and took to hospital. On her favourite felt shawl, a faded green and lilac piece with wild snaking threads throughout it, a blob of toothpaste remained.

My mother brushed her teeth twice a day in hospital, leaning against the sink for support with her face close to the mirror, with effort. She still bothered to floss in full knowledge that she wouldn't survive another few months and her teeth would burn out of her jaw at cremation. The blob was five years old. A memento of her last days in hospital. My hand flew up to cover my heart. Oh Mum.

Over ten years of recurring breast cancer my mother tried intravenous Vitamin C injections, an alternative chemotherapy from Germany delivered at a sophisticated-appearing centre situated across the beach in Manly, Sydney, psychic surgery, diets, practising a visual meditation where you rid yourself of your disease, and emotional work, believing the cancer might have roots in her deeply held sense of trauma as an ill-placed adopted child. She left her academic career in Sydney and moved to the Northern Rivers, a place she valued for its lifestyle and expanse of beautiful beaches and sub-tropical rainforest.

It didn't work.

Like some death knell it struck again every two years. In 1997 she had recurrent local disease in the same breast and underwent another lumpectomy. Again she refused adjuvant radiotherapy. That year we spent Christmas with friends in Canberra. The healing wound became infected and opened up on Christmas Eve. I packed the wound with gauze as nurses had shown me to do, but the situation was beyond my abilities. Mum and her best friend, Tess, spent the rest of Christmas Day in accident and emergency with a residential doctor who appeared to be 11.

In 1998 the cancer reared up again around the time of her birthday – same breast. This time Mum had a mastectomy and her lymph nodes removed. Prior to surgery I'd called a 'meet' of all her female friends for her birthday, and after a yummy fusion meal in Byron Bay I went around the table and asked everyone what they thought Mum should do: lumpectomy or mastectomy. Mum had agreed to follow her friends' advice even if she didn't want to. The hands-down decision was for a mastectomy. Mum's health insurance hadn't kicked in yet so I did a call to alms with all our friends and family, and generated enough to take the sting out of the operational costs of surgery in a private hospital. As Mum's oncologist was private, so too was surgery.

My mother had non-typical secondary breast cancer – it had metastasised to her ovaries and part of the addendum of her stomach. The surgical response to this was a radical hysterectomy. The year was 2000. After surgery she commenced hormone therapy with Letrozole (another aromatase inhibitor).

In 2003 it went to her bones. At this point it had spread to the lining of her skull.

In 2004 it went to her liver – the seat of her terminal diagnosis. My mother's oncologist put her on a low dose of Taxotere and Adriamycin from August 2004 to September 2004. And again – with a different regimen – from November 2004 to January 2005.

In 2005 she underwent several months of palliative chemotherapy under a lovely palliative care doctor based out of Greenslopes Private Hospital (up until this time Mum had been seen by doctors at the Wesley Hospital) who reduced the tumour in her liver and doubled the length of time she'd been given to live, which was roughly six months.

When my mother was first diagnosed she read a lot of the cancer literature. She shoved the German alternative chemotherapy trial results under the noses of her oncologist and treating doctors. She wanted them to see there were alternatives to their wisdom.

In consultations with specialist doctors I took notes while Mum talked. I asked a few questions, but overall I remained in the role of dutiful daughter. At 22 I didn't seek out the cancer literature myself. I trusted my mother to know what she was talking about as she always had – or so I'd believed. But in hindsight, and with the knowledge gleaned from my own illness, I'm amazed at the choices she made. At the way she played Russian roulette with her own life. Of course, she didn't see it this way.

As I've said, I believe fear played a huge role in directing her away from conventional medicine. When you walk into an oncology unit and get plugged into cytotoxic drugs, you are truly a cancer patient and your life is on the line for all to see – by you, most clearly of all.

I helped Mum in post-surgery recoveries, but I didn't live nearby. I would ultimately return home. If I'd stayed closer geographically, would her decisions have been different?

When we talked about her impending death she said that I got as close as possible to knowing her without being her. She trusted me to give doctors the okay to increase her morphine or to give instructions to turn off a life support machine, if it got that far. And it did. Three days before Mum died, two doctors talked to me outside her room.

We're going to increase the morphine to reduce your mother's discomfort. Do you know what this means?

They both looked into my eyes for comprehension. I knew exactly what this meant. Euthanasia is hotly debated in Australia. Officially it isn't used, but in practice it is, mainly for those in hospital dying. Doctors regularly assist them to go without pain, and more quickly.

Do you know what this means?

Yes, I do. Okay. Yes.

Your mother will slip into a coma, which'll likely last three days, then her organs will close down and eventually her lungs will stop working. Soon after we increase her morphine she won't be able to speak with you. If you need to speak with her before she goes into a coma, you should do it now.

In the end my mother was going to die of organ failure brought on by a medically induced coma, not by the creep of cancer's throttling tendrils.

In the last week of Mum's life three Canberran friends had flown up. Ngaire and two others: a psychologist and talented painter with his wife, who worked in promotions and made people welcome as if she'd harnessed some of the sun's warmth.

The day they all went to see Mum in hospital, I took them out to lunch on a cliff top overlooking a sparkling Gold Coast beach. I'd driven down that morning with Ngaire and hadn't had much time alone with my mother. Before I left to drive them to a seafood lunch I leant over the hospital bed and hugged Mum tightly and she said, You don't have to go.

I smiled and replied, I know, but they've come all this way and I should take them out.

Mum nodded then hugged me again. You're being so brave, my darling.

Not really, I replied, then left for lunch.

These inane words turned out to be the last I ever spoke with my mother. If only I'd known, I would never have taken her friends to lunch. I would've stayed and said all the bottled-up things I realised I wanted to say after she died, like: I loved my childhood, thank you for that, you were a wonderful mother and life teacher, I'm so proud of you and you'll be okay.

When my mother died, so too did my history. I was marooned in the present without a past storyteller – my co-truthteller. Now the only past I had was my own recall of events – no new baby stories or anecdotes. Orphaned to the present.

Three days before Christmas – five years after her death – I put my mother's collection of postcards into a display folder. They dated back to the early 1970s. On the back of a lot of them were scrawled words from men who'd loved my mother. One in particular, a man who'd met her when they were both students doing the extra postal rounds at Christmas, wrote 60 postcards. He also wrote multiple letters which hadn't survived. My mother didn't have much luck in her later relationships but at least she inspired great passion and love in the men she did hold close. No small thing. I remembered when she handed them to me from her stationery drawer and I said, Cool, I can use them.

Don't you dare, she'd replied, these are my collection.

I turned over a postcard of a brightly coloured teddy bear and it was from 'Janette', congratulating Mum on her daughter's arrival into the world. It was addressed to Heather and Roger: this was the first time I'd seen evidence of my parents on the same page, proving, finally, that they had once been a couple in a public way. On another card was a 1920s-inspired art deco image of two women dancing – inside was the message: *Happy 21st, may you be successful in all your endeavours.*

Christmas Day

Thou know'st 'tis common; all that lives must die,
Passing through nature to eternity.

William Shakespeare, *Hamlet*

Next of kin? asked a triage nurse, as I stood swaying with nausea. I was having an allergic reaction to prawns, one week after my mother's death. It was close to midnight on New Year's Eve. *Next of kin?*

My mother died at 8 p.m. on Christmas Day. For all the years I'd put her name down, automatically, on all official documents. I could no longer do that.

B, my partner, is my next of kin. I'd responded with a full sentence to reconfirm and sound it out in my head for the first time – *my mother was dead.* My father, and every other remaining relative, lived in England. I felt more than orphaned. I felt the weight of my mother's death rest again on my chest. *Motherless.*

I supported my mother with my physical presence as she died. I prepared her Tibetan chants for death (on CD) with a mantra placed over her heart, as advised by a Tibetan Buddhist nun, Thubten. My mother took refuge in the Buddha in the last year of her life, which is a ritual similar to baptism for Christians.

I touched her one last time. Holding her head next to mine: cheek to cheek. You can go now, Mum. I love you. I kissed her warm forehead and felt her short curly hair. To look at my mother was like looking at a part of me – I knew her better than any other human being.

Two hours before my mother's death we'd taken a break at a coastal lookout. The sun was setting and a flock of birds was returning home. Tess took a photo of B and me sharing a kiss; it's still on our fridge. On the drive back to the hospital an ultra-real glow of burning orange illuminated the inside of our car as the sun finally went down. Every moment in that car trip back to her bedside felt like levitating. I was encased in a film so otherworldly that any question directed at me was muffled, as if it was spoken through a thin wall.

I entered Mum's room expecting her to be in the same position. She wasn't. A nurse had set a sheet so that it no longer rested upon her body, but over the bed's sidebars. The nursing staff had turned Mum onto her right side. Music was playing, not hers, but the nurse's. The room was cocooned. The curtains were drawn, the lights turned low. I stood as close to Mum as possible, searching her face for her presence, my chest wracked with sobs. My mother was dying, the time had come, and I was scared.

A nurse came up behind us and said something about making her comfortable. It was a clear message that my mother was going. The nurse stepped delicately into our grief and out of it.

At that stage I only wished for Mum to die in grace, something she'd wanted. I didn't think of what it meant to no longer share a cup of tea or hear her voice.

The last year of my mother's life was a real 'journey'. Heather, what cleansing! Thubten had said in response to the year's difficulties and the awareness Mum brought to her impending death. To which Mum had playfully responded, Yeah, great. What's Buddhism ever done for me?

I sat in a chair next to the bed, staring directly at Mum's mouth and face. B was next to me and Tess was on the other side of the bed, watching Mum's ribcage. We kept vigil, remained silent and didn't touch, as in Buddhist practice.

Breathe in. The sound was audible as her life force struggled in one of its last remaining activities. She was Cheyne–Stokes breathing: her ribcage would expand in a deep breath then deflate like it was sinking to the bottom of a pool.

Breathe out. I sighed with relief as my mother's lungs kept working.

Breathe in. I didn't capture her on video for her future grandchildren.

Breathe out. My mother was still in the room with me.

Breathe in. The gap between in-breath and out was growing.

Breathe out. Mum's face was white and still but her presence was warm.

Breathe in. Her grey-black curls framed her face gently. She appeared peaceful.

Breathe out. I wondered if she knew where she was.

Breathe in. Mum had taken refuge in the Buddha from a Tibetan high priest. Was it helping her to leave life?

Breathe out. All financial loose ends were tied up.

Breathe in. Mum knew I had a wonderful partner, whom she'd dubbed the golden boy.

Breathe out. She was a great mother.

Breathe in. *Where are you going, Mum?*

Breathe out.

Tess and I looked up at one another and half-smiled in recognition.

My mother was dead.

She was so brave. It was easy to focus on the complexity of Mum's emotions and panicked fears in her relationships with men, but when big stuff happened she was calm; she was strong. She died with dignity and grace, as she'd wanted. I was so proud of her.

Worrying: am I on the right path?

It's okay to keep hearing your worries, so long as you
stop talking to them. Shun them like a double-crossed Quaker.

Imagine how quiet it would be, like shutting off the droning ocean.
That's how our parasites must feel about our hearts.
What a racket, all that pumping. shut up shut up

Jennifer Michael Hecht, 'My Hero'

If only I could shut up this gnawing doomsday script in my head. After I finished my cancer treatments and I was given the all clear, I flipped from *I'm cancer free* to *My chances of remaining cancer free are low* anxieties. I had a whirly rumination track that repeated conversations or thoughts – including one I wished I'd never had.

When I was 21 I decided to meet with my mum's psychic and have a session. Her home was in the Blue Mountains. At the time my mother was living in North Richmond at the base of the mountains. It's a small town on the flat near Bells Line of Road, a main road up into the mountains. When you drive up this steep road the bellbirds call to one another across dense trees.

At this time Mum was still a lecturer at the University of Western Sydney. In a few months she'd end the disastrous relationship she had with a faculty professor who loved porn. And she'd also be diagnosed with cancer.

The psychic seemed a rational woman with a stable family life and comfortable home. She was grounded and kind. In fact, that year she stopped doing readings to focus on her art, as according to Mum she found the responsibility and burden of her psychic connection too much. I have a dim memory of Mum saying the psychic didn't want to tell people about their futures anymore. Had she really been able to, anyway?

I sat down in her room; the psychic connected with her guide then started the tape recorder. I have a copy of this conversation on tape, moulding away in a box under the house. She told me that I'd make a wonderful mother. There was a hint of sadness in her voice, which I wished I'd asked about. I remember just thinking, *Yeah, I know I will.* Nothing wrong with this; I liked this information about good mothering. Then she said that at around 40 years of age I'd say *That's enough* to mothering and write poetry. At the time I just shrugged and thought, *Cool, I have kids, not sure about poetry though.* Next I asked about the children's father and she said I'd spend the rest of my life with him.

Back in the cancer present this conversation played again and again in my mind: the comments about poetry and the rest of my life. I projected my son's situation onto it and questioned, *Was this destined? Could I have changed this?* I dropped this thinking quick smart.

The thing that kept bugging me was poetry at 40. I was terrified, as if my life depended upon it, that I wouldn't get to write again until I was 40 or, worse, that my writing would lead nowhere. Plus I was no poet.

When I was told, You have invasive ductal carcinoma, I didn't feel I'd achieved what I was capable of or wanted out of life. My mother felt the same.

Throughout recurring bouts of breast cancer Mum struggled with letting go of her near-complete PhD so that she could focus upon her joy, which was felting. I used to joke that if she could have felted her PhD, it would have been completed in one year.

Mum stretched out her PhD until it flaked at the edges. She died with a chapter and a half left before submission. So much of her research and years spent thinking and writing went unrewarded. Mum was supposed to write her PhD while living in the Northern Rivers, recovering from cancer. Five years on from my mother's death I was about to pick up my master's after finishing major cancer treatment. I didn't want to die with unfinished work. I didn't want to die at all.

Physical intimacy: what is sexuality?

The saying is true: 'The empty vessel makes the greatest sound.'

William Shakespeare, *Henry V*

No one – not even breast care nurses – told me my vagina might shrink to the size of a raisin. When my oncologist explained the barrage of drugs required to suppress my body's natural production of oestrogen, I dived into the literature on sudden menopause. Anything vagina-related took third place or lower in medical literature and personal accounts of psychosexual issues for women post-treatment. The focus was on hot flushes and low libido.

The heat surges I'd covered; the dry martini I had not.

In daily life you're rarely aware of your vagina, snug and warm between your legs, unless, of course, it's titillated or develops thrush. However, after chemotherapy I noticed a chafing sensation. Or worse, after my first forays into riding a bike, a sore feeling, as if I'd been cut. Basically she had a dry throat and thin skin that only false lubrication could quench.

I returned to the vagina literature. There were a few

lubricants recommended for women with hormone-positive breast cancer. I only needed the occasional KY to make myself comfortable but there were others: Replens was an oestrogen-free, long-lasting moisturiser. Sylk was a natural personal lubricant that helped end the 'dry spells', as it said on their home page. Or there was Astroglide personal lubricant. This lube had the most interesting backstory.

Dan Wray stumbled on the product while working on the cooling system of a space shuttle at Edwards Air Force Base in 1977. He tried to remove the oil from anhydrous ammonia and ended up with this substance. As a joke he gave a colleague some in a glass jar. The colleague later returned, red-cheeked, for a refill. This was the beginning of his multi-million-dollar affair with gliding gel. What I wanted to know was: the caustic ammonia bit was gone, right?

Part of saying goodbye to my sex drive and part of my sexual identity as a woman was recalling my sexy 20s, when I did experiment and have sexual partners. My body was very fit and healthy from rock climbing, and I revelled in sharing its pleasures.

Chemotherapy and my maintenance drug regimen made me blasé about a diminishing sex drive. I never thought this possible. Who? Me? My falling libido meant I didn't care that it was lowered because, well, it was lowered.

In a way it came as a relief. Our sex drive can *drive* so much in our daily interactions. An attraction at a party can lead to an animated conversation, and jealousy in a partner. Now, it was like I'd stepped off the hormonal needs cycle and stood back like a great-grandmother with all of 'that stuff' behind her. Another focus drove my interactions.

Do you still find me attractive? I made a funny face at B. We were sitting on our click-clack wooden couch in the lounge room.

Of course, he replied and smiled. The three casement windows with bobbled glass let in a subdued light from the overcast day outside.

I pointed to my Hollywood boobs and said, Even with these?

B reflected for a minute then said, It's different, I focus elsewhere now.

Okay. This was fine with me. Are you worried that we might become a no-sex couple? We won't always be one. It's just that I'm not feeling like a sexy lady, I babbled on.

Sure. B gave a *Don't be silly* look and added, All couples go through highs and troughs in their lives together. I know we'll get sexy again. I don't feel that interested at the moment either.

Right. He was so logical and so assured. I wondered if B's sense of stability in relationships was because his parents had stayed together and worked side by side as creators of substantial gardens most of their adult lives. When it came to relationships my emotional ground was much rockier. I knew that relationships failed and marriages ended, and that sometimes passion turned violent. I once witnessed my mother thrown against a flimsy wooden cupboard. It had creaked like it was cracking. I was nine, and raced up the stairs to my private attic bedroom that I loved so much. Mum had raced up the stairs too and found me cowering under the duvet.

Look what you've done! she screamed down to her circus ringmaster.

She had thrown the first punch.

Now I was a eunuch woman, and focussed on other things to do in bed, like reading as much as possible. Flippancy aside, the relief of the situation reminded me of what it had been like to find a life partner. The energy involved in trying to meet *the right one* or partner up once you did went into other life pursuits, like focussing on study, career decisions or home building. The same with diminishing sexual desire.

At the time I was resigned – this was *how it was going to be*. And later, when my desire for B returned, it stemmed from a different place. Just like the brain attempts to create different neural networks after cerebral damage, my desire for my partner was top-down, head first instead of lust first. The arousal came from my love for him and the way he smelt. As the comedian Robin Williams joked, you want someone who gives good mind. The rest follows.

But my vagina itself? It was not dried-grape size, but it wasn't yoga queen either. For several years the elasticity of my vaginal tissue was reduced because of low oestrogen, and this made full sexual intercourse almost impossible, and extremely painful without synthetic lubrication. I'd spoken with quite a few women about this side effect of their treatment and one woman in particular introduced me to plastic vaginal expanders provided by her radiation nurses. I called the hospital straight away, leaving a message with a male oncologist standing in for mine. The message read:

> Want to get my portacath out so I can return to New Zealand and trek with my family without worrying about getting it flushed or having my pack's straps irritate it. I also want some vaginal expanders as I'm shrinking.

As getting an appointment and seeing my oncologist or any medical specialist took a while, I'd taken matters into my own hands. I decided that as my body was fit from the gym post-chemo I should similarly get my vagina in shape post-chemo too. I went online and found a women-focussed sex aid site and bought a toy. It resembled a large, somewhat dented U with one side smallish and the other side bigger. And it was purple. I was going to practise until perfect like all good devotees. Smirks aside, I needed to get her adequately stretched again if I wanted a full sexual life. At the time there was no motivation, as it basically hurt like I was being injured. Eventually, though, it worked pretty well, so I upgraded to a waterproof vibrator.

Another trick I'd heard about was to pop a Vitamin E capsule inside you daily to lubricate the walls of your vagina. I didn't need to try this at that point. Sex had re-entered my life, but all the surgery and particularly drugs had aged me in ways I never could have foretold.

Within another year I had to take a proactive response to my thinning 'skin' and tried the MonaLisa Touch: a laser treatment for vaginal atrophy (the treatment came into being because allegedly half of all women eventually experience this). One female gynaecologist's website said it was pain free, which is rubbish, as my male gynaecologist lathered me in topical anaesthetic before using the metal, tubular probe. You walk out of the rooms with a pad in your pants like you're a menstruating woman again, complete with spotting.

My gynaecologist was in communication with the Italian developer of the probe about designing one to reach the scar tissue left behind in a woman's vault (the real term) when the cervix is removed during a radical hysterectomy. Currently, the laser goes sideways along the canal of the vagina, but doesn't hit the end, which I needed because that was where my particular pain was coming from. He thought a nerve might have got trapped up in the scar tissue. He'd performed laparoscopic surgery on women – going in and recutting the vault closing to help his patients maintain the ability to have intercourse.

From what I know, the MonaLisa Touch came about during a gynaecological plastic-surgery conference in Italy. Scientists and gynaecologists got talking about laser treatment for taking wrinkles out of rich women's faces. One man asked the question *What about putting wrinkles back in?* – thinking this might work in a woman's vaginal walls. And that's what the MonaLisa Touch does. It stimulates collagen in your connective tissues to put folds (rugae) back into the wall, so they're flexible and develop normal mucosa again – all things a functioning vagina needs.

So I put my hand up to be a guinea pig for the external probe, which normally does the labia only but could be trained straight ahead, and therefore hit the end of my vault, where the scar tissue lay. I did a lot of calm breathing and sweating as the gynaecologist worked this odd-shaped probe into me to reach the scarring in my vault. The process included me with a hand mirror checking out the white spots left behind after the lasering.

Imagine a thick circular probe that goes square and has two tongs on the end like you'd use to carefully flip tofu on a BBQ, and that's what I got up me. I actually felt a vaginal achievement on walking out of the procedure – my adrenaline waning.

But what of the vagina at the end of all these breast cancer treatments?

I met a breast care nurse and survivor who'd received a Churchill Fellowship to study survivorship issues in America. She put me on to drinking a capful of apple cider vinegar in water every day. She too noticed, after treatments for breast and gynaecological cancer and being on Arimidex, that she didn't smell the same. Her pH was out. Mine too. No longer.

The rabbit hole of sexual intimacy post–aggressive cancer treatments was and generally is not discussed by medical professionals advising you, the patient, on everything that will keep you alive. As survivorship increases, wonderfully, so too will the numbers of women (young to old) living with cancer as a chronic disease or with no sign of disease. This leaves a gap of care for those who want to live well post-cancer.

In my undergraduate study, my lecturer in philosophical psychology described the female orgasm and how the cervix pulsed in and out of the vaginal canal like a chicken picking up seeds (read sperm) off the ground. Chicken-beak analogy aside, orgasm quality is reduced, quite a bit, by having your cervix removed. No one talked about this. I couldn't find it in medical literature, or in breast cancer stories. Why is the vagina and women's sexual use of it so omitted? If a man's testicle is removed or his penis operated on, there'd be a lot of conversation about sexual function. Not so for women. Yes, our sexual organs are 'hidden' from view, but does it go deeper than this?

Women's sexual desire isn't as important perhaps, or rather talking about women and their own desire, separate from men's desire for them, is still not de rigueur?

But for all the stretching and lube and lasering, whether you maintain your pH or put a READY silicone capsule inside yourself for increased lubrication, or all of the above: ultimately, you are not the same.

Hope: can you learn to live well in conversation with death?

O spare me, that I may discover strength, before I go hence, and be no more.

Psalm 39:13 (KJV)

I walked into Dr Theile's office on a brisk July morning with no nipples, and an hour and a half later I had some. They were not giving any peekaboo action through my shirt yet, of course – when I peered down my top all I saw was two 20-centimetre blood stains under waterproof dressings. The dressings stayed on a week.

I opted to have the nipple ruffles performed under local anaesthetic, to avoid a general anaesthetic and hospital stay. It was painless, and took the length of a good lunch with friends. I didn't have to enter the hospital system and more importantly have my brain and body shut down for a minor surgical procedure. No nausea and no pea-souper.

While I was on the operating table, Dr Theile, his nurse and I talked about Charlie Teo – a renowned (some say notorious) Australian neurosurgeon. I'd just read *Life in His Hands*, about Dr Teo's treatment of a young pianist with a hemangiopericytoma brain tumour. These tumours originate in membrane covering the brain tissue and are classed as malignant because the recurrence rate is high and they grow fast. They mostly occur in young men.

My plastic surgeon and Dr Teo met as registrars in Queensland. Dr Teo had sat in a coffee room in full bike leathers, with a thumping 1000-cc motorbike parked outside, after riding up from Sydney. Dr Theile liked his openness and thought him a genuinely nice guy.

According to some neurosurgeons Charlie Teo operated on patients others classed as inoperable. Some of his surgeries resulted in quicker deaths and unpleasant final days before the brain tumour took its toll. My discussion with Dr Theile that day was about hope. Dr Teo provided hope when others didn't, even if the surgery was so risky the person's life might end in the operating theatre.

If you have a doctor willing to risk a procedure that might give you longer on the earth, and you're fully briefed on the consequences if the operation fails, then having the choice to hope, beyond medical doubts, is worthy in my eyes.

American haematologist–oncologist and author Dr Jerome Groopman put it like this:

> My place is to provide choice and understanding. To hope under the most extreme circumstances is an act of defiance … that permits a person to live his life on his own terms. It is part of the human spirit to endure and give a miracle a chance to happen.

Dr Groopman said that what was once a miraculous turn-around from likely death is now more commonplace. The advancements in chemotherapy treatments have provided hope in areas previously thought hopeless.

The reason I was lighter and happier when I woke up without my breasts was that hope had flooded back into my room. I finally dared to think *I might survive this.*

Several months before my mother died the palliative chemotherapy she received had shrunk the metastatic tumours in her liver. The reason my mother gave palliative chemotherapy a try was to sustain her life long enough to tie up loose ends like a failing marriage as well as to have as long as possible with me. Her then husband left the house with their two untrained wire-haired fox terriers and went on a road trip. An escape for him and us. He said he did it for my mother, knowing his presence and behaviour were unacceptable and disturbing. He also hitched his wagon to another unsuspecting woman, advertising himself on a dating website as a widower before my mother was dead. *Love me, love my dogs* was his by-line.

When I entered her home to become her full-time carer, she had, in her own words, been sent home to die. There was no further treatment offered, and no arrangements made for hospice services, or even any information about support services in her area. In the Northern Rivers you had to drive to the Gold Coast or Brisbane for appointments with medical specialists. I wasn't informed about travel or accommodation assistance for overnight stays if my mother was too ill to sit in a car after a hard day on the drugs. Once, our car broke down and we had to wait for roadside assistance. There was no hope of a recovery and she'd been given roughly a year to live if she made the palliative chemotherapy trips. A year after my own diagnosis I became a cancer patient advocate with CanSpeak Queensland to correct some of these ways in which the health system failed people diagnosed with cancer, especially those dying of the disease.

One morning Mum sat up in bed and in a chirpy voice said, You never know, a miracle might happen. I could still be cured. She smoothed the creased bed linen across her lap.

Well ... I started, then softened my tone to sound gentle. I just don't want you to have false hope. Your cancer is classed as terminal.

Mum looked down, making a face like a child who'd been chastened. Tea then? She brought her chin up.

Coming up! and I exited stage right to the kitchen.

Why did I not have more fun with it? Make the conversation lighter? Instead I quashed her levity.

In *Life in His Hands* a New Zealand journalist, Michael Bartrom, was refused a referral to Dr Charlie Teo on the grounds that his doctors didn't believe anything more could be done. Bartrom considered their attitude amoral; he could only imagine a future with himself still in it.

We all have this vision and wish to be the ones sitting in a future photograph surrounded by friends and family instead of the absent one in the picture. Hope offered in the hands of medicine and its latest findings lets us die knowing we've done our best, or that the choice was ours to refuse further treatment and a handshake made with death instead.

Unfortunately my nipples didn't stay in place. Instead of nipple ruffles I got nipple pimples. The waterproof dressing was not so waterproof. I left the dressing on for several days as advised and when I changed it the wound area was infected. I guessed the water trailed in along my mastectomy scar, because the second waterproof dressing (which was said to absorb fluid up to ten times its weight) allowed water to sneak in also. My friend, an experienced wound-care nurse, said that the infection was likely there before the dressing became wet.

With the infection the wound's stitching spread apart and in effect undid/unzipped itself and the neat job performed by my surgeon. The result of all this was that my previously pert nipple skin ruffles were flattened; they were goners.

Dr Theile told me to allow the wound to dry out. On seeing the infection he quickly announced, We'll get them looking good, don't worry. Then he proceeded to discuss skin grafts, preferably taken near an existing scar to mask the graft site.

I blanked out the entire conversation about skin grafting. I didn't want more hassle for something that was between B and me only. If we could live with the current result then they were staying as they were.

After the wounds healed they were minuscule rises on each breast, which I decided to leave alone so that I could wear camisoles under tops and forget the bra. Moreover, if I wore a tight-fitting top the small bumps showed as flattened nipples would under a solid bra. In short, my nipples could fake well enough for me.

Post-it all emotions:
does stress cause cancer?

... neural networks are sensitive and, once formed, are prone to repetition. In neuroscience, one of the first ideas I learned, no doubt made memorable by the convenient rhyme, was Hebb's law: 'Neurons that fire together wire together.' The more I shake, the more likely it is that I'll shake in the future.

Siri Hustvedt, *The Shaking Woman*

I had elevator emotions. They sat inside my chest in some sort of shaft. It was easy for the emotions to descend to the stomach's ground level, a solemn interior with little light.

I clocked the elevator emotions as they descended: the nausea after a general anaesthetic bruised my outlook (it tingled in my chest); my son wasn't babbling or saying words at 18 months (it weighed heavily at the top of my gut); I could actually die from breast cancer (bang on the bottom).

With the physical sensations of my emotions heading south, my face dropped its hold on fine muscles around my mouth, which was normally quick to smile. All of me wanted to pile up on the floor and Wizard of Oz out of there into another place in the world where I could be someone else.

In the blue of depression I smelt red. My blood was close to the surface. I feared an unthinking moment with a knife or tall building would spill it. I wanted to die to this life and rebirth into another. Not for real, you see, just out of the pain of it. The sickening flatness of no hope.

I'd thought these lows were all behind me. After the wounds healed from my double mastectomy and immediate reconstruction, I practised living in the room. What I meant by this was that when thoughts frightened me – of dying from cancer, or Celso's future and mine as a full-time carer – I drew my mind back to what was in front of me. For three months, post-chemotherapy, I'd consciously done this. The positive effect was noticeable.

Celso was in the corner holding up a toy, and stamping his feet in joy as a good-morning hello. B had just brought in cucumbers, basil, asparagus and lettuce from our formal vegetable garden. I had half an hour with my white tea indulgence and an Isabel Dalhousie novel before my son required plugging in to feed.

The immediate reality was almost always better than my dark future imaginings. Things were generally okay. I had hope.

It took two days of nausea and bad diarrhoea to put me back on the elevator heading south. It didn't happen like that before breast cancer or before my high-needs baby arrived. Back then, nausea was from a good meal turned bad or in my first trimester of pregnancy, and it evaporated under the warm, hopeful thoughts of the joy I'd get from my bright, sparkling baby to be.

But now I'd picked up Celso's stomach bug, so for two days I was ill and running to the toilet all the time.

B and I walked to the local organic markets on Sundays with Celso in the buggy, which took 15 minutes. To the right of the bike path the tidal Breakfast Creek flowed out through the mangroves, which lined both sides of the river and were several trees deep. I often superimposed a crocodile's head popping up near the water's edge, though without the ticking clock. To the left were large playing fields and a dog off-leash area, with a couple of Welsh terriers and a golden retriever sallying about. The sun was out, it wasn't too hot and we had money in our pockets for breakfast. It was really quite lovely – externally.

I found deep truth in this throwaway line: if you have your (full) health you have everything. Often during the intense illness phase of chemotherapy I could not imagine happiness returning to my life.

I pulled through the sick stuff knowing it would end. In the throes of a particularly bad night I understood how chronically ill people acknowledged they wanted out – they wanted death.

These two days surprised me in how suddenly a deluge of sadness rushed in when there was nausea. The queasiness was a body memory, triggering my dark days on chemotherapy. I was haunted by the chemicals.

We did the normal Sunday-market buying of bread and a coffee for B, chai for me, and saying hello to regulars we bumped into every week while Celso played in the sandpit. Our exchanges with people left me flat. Usually I was animated with people and enjoyed others' company, but not during these two nauseous days. The hard-won enjoyment of food after chemotherapy deserted me again. I couldn't fill up with good feeling from anything, not even my family. Celso likely made me smile at something or I'd give him a hug on the spur of the moment because I loved him, but the spark was smote.

When the nausea abated I got sudden buzzes of great feeling: I was alive. The simple truth of this exhilarated me. The adrenaline of dodging a bullet. In May 2009 I had aggressive breast cancer. A year on, I didn't. I feared challenging the gods with the assuredness that I was a cancer-free person; that might jinx me.

The minutiae of everyday living didn't seem so everyday. I'd spent a lot of time at home over the last few years: caring for my mother, supporting my partner while he worked and studied, studying for my MA, caring for Celso, and then recuperating from breast cancer while caring for Celso. At times cabin fever reached boiling temperature and I wanted to run screaming, not for the hills but for intellectual stimulation. This had quietened down after chemotherapy.

After my master's panel interview, before Celso was born, where I presented my thesis and argued its worth, a fellow candidate said I had a bit of the obsessive about me. I'd planned all my slides meticulously. She was right; I did, hidden somewhere deep.

In late adolescence I'd pass objects like a handrail or doorknob and if I didn't touch it the right way I'd go back and touch it again, for example running my hand along the full length of a shiny, wooden handrail. I also disliked people talking in abbreviations. I tended to use the full term or name before moving on in the conversation, for example if someone asked me, Could you buy some tommies? I'd likely respond, How many tomatoes do you want?

At 19, when I was studying and living in Lismore, I confessed my obsessive-type touch-retouch thing to the GP I was involved with; he said I was just wanting to get things right or feel my way in the world. It clicked instantly, and I stopped going back to hold the doorknob the right way, and other oddities. It was a similar light-bulb 'got it' when Mum took me for a long drive to tell me she loved me after she'd guessed that I was still drug-affected after a rave at 16 years of age. I stopped experimenting with drugs that instant: point blank.

A cancer diagnosis made me stop and look closely at how I was living: did I do anything to bring this on? I was ready to change anything, right away.

The first questions my breast surgeon asked were: Do you smoke? (No.) Do you get regular exercise? (Yes.) Do you drink alcohol? (The very occasional glass or two of wine.) Do you eat well? (Yes – we bought mostly organic food, milk and meat products.)

The main reasons for my getting breast cancer at 35 appeared to be genetic ones. There was talk – in literature, informal conversations between friends, and research involving women newly diagnosed with breast cancer – of stress being a contributing factor to the development of cancer. All I knew was that the only environmental factor that I could name as a possible contributor was stress. In caring for my mother and my son I experienced a lot of it. However, I didn't blame stress for my cancer, but rather I believed I inherited the tendency towards cancer from my mother.

Stress comes in two forms: from working hard or from a situation you have no control over. The latter was what allegedly could dupe you.

Scientist Dr Elizabeth Blackburn won the Nobel Prize for Physiology and Medicine in 2009 for her research into telomeres, the protective caps on the ends of chromosomes. She worked with psychologists on telomeres, stress and meditation. It appeared that she had proven a mind–body connection. Her Australian voice with its US West Coast twang came to me over the radio in my kitchen. She said, In my lab, we're finding that psychological stress actually ages cells, which can be seen when you measure the wearing down of the tips of the chromosomes, those telomeres.

Dr Blackburn's work helped us understand why breast cancer cells divide without normal control. Her work also had a lot to say about bad stress and good stress. She said:

> … there's all sorts of good stress; I just came back from the gym and believe me I stressed my body and I'm incredibly happy. And so this is a stress where you rise to a challenge, you control it and that's something that we're evolved to do very well, you know, the zebra runs away from the lion and so forth. So we can do all the kind of acute reaction to stress and acute stress situations very, very well. But what happens is that in the long term if the stress situation is something that the individual sees always as a threat or continues to see threatening rather than challenging situations, doesn't identify resources to cope, etc. etc. That's the kind of stress that's been long known to have clear clinical outcomes which are poor outcomes. So that's been known from a number of studies for a number of years. But the part of the puzzle that we added in was that we said well let's look at ageing of cells right at the heart of the cell's decision to renew or not and that's the

decision that a cell makes based on many things. But one of them is whether it feels its genetic material is at risk, and if the telomere is run down the cell will stop operations and will not self-renew.

So we looked and said, does the running down of telomeres with ageing have any relationship to stress? And we found in one case a causal direction that the chronic stress was, we think, causally related to the telomeres running down. In other words – the longer the number of years a person was under an objective stressor … the more years the person was under stress the worse was their shortening of their telomeres over and above what normally would happen just in the normal course of ageing. So that to us was very interesting, because it said somehow chronic stress is having effects on the brain, which we clearly know, which is having effects on physiology in all sorts of ways, and one end result of that is that the telomeres are running down and our cells are losing the ability to renew.

The attention to detail of my obsessive tendencies re-focussed on a healthy diet and exercise, as the stress of caring for my mother was behind me but the stress of having cancer and a high-needs child was smack in front of me. I was doing everything possible on the conventional medical front, so I turned to my Self. What opportunities did I have to improve? The first thing that raised its sugary head was chocolate. Oh to swim in Willy Wonka's chocolate stream. I loved the stuff. I cut back on my consumption.

My breast surgeon recommended I read a well-researched book about new ways of eating to support your body, written by a clinical professor of psychiatry, Dr David Servan-Schreiber, who'd had two brain tumours. He kept cancer at bay for years longer than his prognosis. A friend of his had asked how he was treating his terrain: the body's underlying health, separate to medical intervention. At the time he was working so hard at the hospital he had a lunch of chilli con carne, a bagel and a can of Coke. He reflected later how this was an explosive combination of white flour and sugar, together with animal fats loaded with omega-6s, hormones and environmental toxins. He had also reduced his exercise and dropped his interest in meditation. He had done nothing to look after himself – to support his body to reduce his chance of relapse.

After reading his section on diet I had another light-bulb realisation. It was like the decision to stop re-touching door handles and to stop taking ecstasy. This time I immediately excluded all pastries and fried food, in addition to the hot chips I'd already eliminated, from my diet. Easy. I haven't touched any since and never will again. I modified main meals to include more steamed greens like Brussels sprouts, and I took up green tea to replace my English tea with milk habit. (I converted back to English tea six years on as the taste was too good to miss.) With chocolate I reached for 70 per cent cocoa, which was higher in nutrients and therefore better for you, or I didn't eat it at all.

I no longer 'did' exercise as a by-product of my passion for rock climbing, where getting rip-roaring fit went with the challenge of solving a difficult crux (the tricky part of a climb). Instead I tripped through the local door of a gymnasium before the sun rose to attend get-fit classes and later became a road cyclist to remain fit. I wasn't developing a skill to aid a lifestyle choice, but I was fit again.

Pink bits: can a doctor–patient relationship help heal you?

In a novel by Joy Williams called State of Grace, *a character says, 'There must be something beyond love. I want to get there.' The sick man has got there: He's at a point where what he wants most from people is not love but an appreciative critical grasp of his situation, what is known now in the literature of illness as 'empathetic witnessing.' The patient is always on the brink of revelation, and he needs an amanuensis.*

Anatole Broyard, 'The Patient Examines the Doctor'

One year on from my mastectomy and reconstruction I entered Dr Theile's office to cross one last t. I was getting my areolas tattooed. It was the finale to a year-long process to reconstruct my breasts.

What's the dye made out of? I asked.

Dr Theile was leaning over me on the surgical table, penning where he'd place the areolas on my breast mounds. I don't know, he answered. His nurse was beside him, handing him instruments.

Great!

165

The nurse smiled down at me. I'd come across a little harsher than I meant.

He continued, But the cosmetic tattooing done on women's faces is a vegetable dye, so it wears off eventually in case they don't like it.

That's a good idea. The white lights of the room and overhead lamp meant I could talk more easily with my eyes shut. Eyes open I was distracted by the room.

Dr Theile had me sit up, lean slightly back and then lie down again. He squinted and leant back to see the best place to tattoo my areolas. He was an artist working on a composition. He went over to a long bench and mixed up colours. Do you want browner tones or pinker?

You know, this may sound silly, but I haven't even thought about what colour I'd get them, not once.

He turned and assessed my skin tone. You're more pink.

I nodded. Yes, I agree, pink it is.

The pink ink Dr Theile had worked up was very bright.

I don't want fluorescent areolas.

He chuckled. It's okay – they start out brighter than the end result. After six weeks they fade considerably to flesh tones.

Good ... where did you learn to tattoo? It had interested me ever since I found out that Dr Theile was doing it and not a cosmetic tattooist. I envisioned a white room with surgical students wearing pink aprons and mouth-to-mouth dolls with pierceable skin laid out on tables.

I used to get a medical tattooist to do it, but she became too busy and my patients had to wait too long to complete their reconstructions ... Dr Theile frowned, genuinely distressed at the memory of women's final results getting drawn out. So I started doing it again. Originally I learnt to do it in America. I went over there for further surgical training and they taught me how.

I mumbled, impressed that he had training from highly qualified Americans au fait with cosmetic surgery. All good as far as I was concerned.

Have you read *Direct Red*? I teased.

Dr Theile's back was to me as he put down an instrument. No, I'm very slack.

I had lent the book to him the previous year, hoping he'd find that his early experiences of surgery resonated with the author's – that he could enjoy his highly specific knowledge explored from another's perspective. I figured there were few good surgeon-writers.

His nurse reassured him, That's a bit rough on yourself, isn't it?

You are busy with work, plus you have a family, so it's okay. I softened the tease.

I read *Direct Red: A Surgeon's Story* several months after my mastectomy because my friend Sara had told me there was a mastectomy scene involving a very young woman. I psyched up for it. However, when I read the book's opening line – *I am about to faint. Methylene Blue. Acridine Orange. I have been holding someone's neck open for seven hours* – I was hooked.

The author, Gabriel Weston, gave up a training position in ear, nose and throat surgery in London for a fixed surgical job with less status after meeting Thomas, another woman's baby on a hospital ward. Thomas had inspired her to give herself more time with her own baby. Up until then she hadn't felt an overwhelming need to include more home time. Scenes from the book have stayed in my mind, conjured by her eloquent, haunting words. For example, she assisted on an emergency procedure with a man who'd struggled furiously with the anaesthetist trying to sedate him for an operation on his aortic aneurysm: a swelling or at worst rupture at the aortic wall. The aorta runs out of the left ventricle of the heart and is the largest artery in the body. It goes down into the abdomen, where it heads off into smaller ventricles, common iliacs:

> Looking down, I peered into the trough of Mr Cooke's emptied abdomen, and could see it filling with blood so fast that the outline of the gushing source was visible beneath the red meniscus. Like when you fill a paddling pool with a hose and it's half full and you can see a knuckle shape on the surface just above where the hose is.

The man's situation resonated with the experience of my post-partum haemorrhage, where my internal iliac arteries were tied with dissolving stitches to stop massive blood loss and mortality. Before they'd wheeled me in at 2 a.m. to undergo an emergency operation to save my life and uterus, I had catching pain in my right shoulder, a sign of internal bleeding. I read words of surgeons' and doctors' medical work and thought of the patient's side – my side. I'd had hands like the author's inside me moving my bowel out of the way and stitching me back together again.

Dr Theile knew my body as only a surgeon could. He also had interests outside of plastic surgery, like mountaineering, which had once left him with a broken leg. He liked to travel with his family and read, and I was sure there were other pursuits I had no idea about. He hadn't read the book, but I left the copy with him all the same.

As the American writer, literary critic and editor Anatole Broyard said, I was a patient wanting an amanuensis. This man as surgeon transformed my body. I wanted a two-way acknowledgement. Dr Theile was the best type of medical specialist: someone with a life that informed his humanity.

A new normal:
is how I look important?

I saw my life branching out before me like the green fig tree in the story. From the tip of every branch, like a fat purple fig, a wonderful future beckoned and winked. One fig was a husband and a happy home and children, and another fig was a famous poet and another fig was a brilliant professor, and another fig was Ee Gee, the amazing editor, and another fig was Europe and Africa and South America, and another fig was Constantin and Socrates and Attila and a pack of other lovers with queer names and offbeat professions, and another fig was an Olympic lady crew champion, and beyond and above these figs were many more figs I couldn't quite make out. I saw myself sitting in the crotch of this fig tree, starving to death, just because I couldn't make up my mind which of the figs I would choose. I wanted each and every one of them, but choosing one meant losing all the rest, and, as I sat there, unable to decide, the figs began to wrinkle and go black, and, one by one, they plopped to the ground at my feet.

Sylvia Plath, *The Bell Jar*

A year on I remained cancer free.

In the mirror my once pale chemo-face held more lines. There was a darker hue under my eyes than before. I was more tired than before. My hair was thicker, darker and greyer. The curls returned. My eyes had a clarity to them: there was no rose-coloured glass through which I looked out at life.

When I turned from my face to my body only the chest area revealed my cancer story. The rim of my portacath's ten-cent dimensions no longer thrust out of my skin, making me look vulnerable. In place of the portacath was a 2.5-centimetre red scar.

I had perfect-sized boobs with a hatching of scars where my nipples and areolas used to live. These were the just-discernible remains of my nipple surgery. My pink-tattooed areolas set a target for the eye amid the scars on my chest.

But this was all surface.

On the inside there was so much more to see.

There were significant changes due to menopause. The sudden drop in oestrogen meant my joints ached. My hands were the worst: my knuckles had swollen and stiffened, and had a rheumatoid-arthritis kind of throb.

The dry riverbed patterning on the skin around my nails remained the same, though the tree rings on my nails from my chemotherapy cycles had disappeared. I maintained hand creaming but the skin was drier, rather like dead skin that needed to flake off. Over the rest of my body my skin had lost its moisture. My youthful beauty was fading, fast. My mirror held a mature woman's face – a new beauty – wizened contessa.

In the last visit with my oncologist I enquired about all the joint pain, especially in my right elbow, which hurt to the point of distraction. There was no concern regarding cancer secondaries in my bones because of my symptoms, but rather the pain was likely some slow-healing damage from picking up Celso. I needed a chiropractor to check me out, not an oncologist. Of course, with any pain or bodily discomfort my first thought turned to The Big C.

To calm down and combat the joint pain, I found time and exercise the best panacea. The medicos said that the significant changes due to menopause would ease somewhere between one and five years.

At the end of September a horrible taste, akin to chemo-mouth, returned for a week for no apparent reason. When I didn't have metal mouth I drank and ate a lot of foods rich in anti-oxidants like blueberries, powdered flaxseed with yoghurt (cottage cheese was better to get the flaxseed absorbed but I didn't like its mashed cat-poo taste) on muesli for breakfast, any foods with plenty of garlic, onion and turmeric, and green tea. Dr Servan-Schreiber made an empowering comment about the right foods when he said that there were three meals a day you could use to do something about cancer.

I also returned to some bad food habits around sweet things, and had to rein myself in on cake and biscuit consumption, but desserts are so much more fun to bake, I'd argue.

I got a nasty cold or flu repeatedly, which might've been the cause of my foul mouth. In my second year post-chemotherapy, though, I was proud of my body and what it had coped with. It was not so robust. My strength had slunk away from my hands and arm muscles. I had to hand tight lids to B to open. It used to be the opposite between us.

I got intense night sweats so I was sleep deprived. Because of all of the above my memory was cruddy, really cruddy – to the point that I became seriously concerned about future learning and retention of new information; I thought I was becoming cognitively dumber.

In conversations with strangers or waiting in rooms I could instantly turn red and glisten with sweat. Normally someone doing this is stressed out about something or really embarrassed. But no, I was just heat surging like all the other women before me. People responded simply and really well when I told them I was menopausal and to ignore my sweating self.

I went from a rangy size 8 to 10 to a curvy size 10 and had to exercise regularly to remain so. I didn't notice my reconstructed breasts, apart from an obvious cleavage in low tops. Sometimes, and this seemed odd, I got phantom tingling where my nipples used to be. It reminded me they'd departed. Also the fronts of my breasts were colder to the touch, especially along the scar lines.

Most of the time I loved my body. I was 37 and had experienced many invasive surgeries, from the horror that was Celso's birth to surgery for cancer, and the gruelling regimen of chemotherapy plus daily drug taking to suppress my hormones from attempting to develop another cancer site. I was not perfect in body, but with the return to health and fitness my body felt perfect.

Heightened experience: is life's meaning found in connection with others?

When you climb
out a black well
you are not the same

you come to
in the blue air
with a long sore scar
circling your chest
like the shoreline
of a deep new sea

your hands are webbed
inviting you
to trust yourself
in water stranger
and wilder
than you've ever known

your heart has a kick
your eyes have
a different bite

you have emerged
from some dark wonder
you can't explain

you are not the same

Dorothy Porter, 'Not the Same'

Through the pain of the breast cancer diagnosis and treatment I sank so low. When I went down into the pit of my stomach with my elevator emotions, got out and had a look around, I saw myself as someone who was never going to become an old woman, or achieve things like becoming a writer, or support my family financially in a job which satisfied my desire to care for others in a professional role. The word 'loser' kept springing to mind. After the blackness of this despair, the opposite, light, seared through into my daily existence. I was happy: plain and simple. And alive.

I was alive.

Every Monday in Celso's first few years of life we attended a feeding group, and in the afternoon he and I drove to another place north of the city for speech therapy. Every Tuesday I took him to a 'neurotypical' playgroup for newborns to five-year-olds in a cavernous room in a Baptist church. Every Wednesday he attended an Early Childhood Development Program playgroup for high-needs kids. The children in this group had Down syndrome or other chromosomal disorders; some were autistic and a few had unspecified problems and an overarching diagnosis of Global Developmental Delay (like Celso at the time).

I enjoyed both playgroups, where I spoke with other mothers. I loved it when Celso sparked another child's interest and they played 'hello' or a toddler rolled a ball to him as a means of introducing themselves. In the preschool primordial world of playgroups, morality wasn't known yet and no societal rules were followed; a grumpy boy poured sand over Celso's head and into his eyes because he'd taken hold of the boy's tractor; or a boy with flyaway blond hair and a brain that short-circuited and stopped him from walking properly kissed Celso's hand.

The reverb after being told your child's disabled is numbing. I took a step back with the force of it. Then leant into it. I hoped Celso wasn't so developmentally delayed that he couldn't function in the standard schooling system or socially. My pregnancy fantasies of having a brilliant boy, like his erudite father, were gone. I'd imagined us both teaching him the wonders of life. The genie in the bottle was expectation. I let it out and let it go. There was a risk that Celso's medical issues isolated me from other mothers' experiences of mothering. In high-needs groups I found an understanding of the depth of tiredness and the circuitous, rolling worry associated with caring for these special children. It was the same situation I'd had with my cancer: snap. I went to support groups for young women with breast cancer, and support groups for young women with breast cancer *and* young children.

Come bath time for Celso I'd perch an Astro Boy rubber stamp on the bath's rim: One, two, three. I flicked it into the water. Celso would lean over and shudder with giggles. Red-faced, he grinned with all of his teeth filling up his face. Then he'd pause and pass the rubber stamp up for me to do it again. Flick. Cackle.

Stripped down to its core, my primary focus was still about mothering a child. In this I could connect with other people and their parenting experience. This was important. Writing and mothering went deep for me. The world sat well when I did both: the sun shone, petty things were left, unkind words forgiven. My diagnosis of breast cancer only re-confirmed my need to have both at the centre of my life. This, and my relationship with my partner. All three were essential to my happiness.

Where else to go once you've seen the bottom?

I could comprehend how it was possible to keep sinking: to suicide. I'd never had a true suicidal thought or more importantly a plan before cancer; I wanted life in full Technicolor, please. I had Dorothy Porter's puckered scar across my chest to indicate where I stood in the black well; my heart had a new kick to it; I was not the same. Oh, but for the gods, I was happy again. The minutiae of daily life, mostly domestic, didn't overwhelm me; there was a heightened quality that surrounded my interactions with friends and family. I boarded that plane to see old family friends instead of putting it off, and sent that letter I'd meant to write. The most surprising of all was my complete forgiveness of my father. My relationship with him to date had been my Achilles heel. As a child I suffered a deep sense of abandonment and sense of failure that I wasn't loved by Daddy. Or was this another inheritance? The grief from my mother's primal wound as an adoptee making its way into the next generation's psyche?

My primary school teacher encouraged my poetry, as I've mentioned, and asked one day for me to read out another piece. I did, then promptly burst into tears. I wrote about how, when I was an infant, my family lived in Firle (a tiny village in south England) and that I used to go into the vegetable patch and pull out Mum's carrots, *plunk, plunk*, and that maybe I had also pulled out my father's heart. Marisa, the 'it' girl, a head taller and blonder than any other girls (a future Guess model), put her arm around me. She was kind, sweet and good company. The scene with Marisa was melodramatic but it reflected how my little nine-year-old self felt.

I guarded my heart and words with my father as a young woman, determined to never let him get to me again. But I failed. In the week I was very ill and hospitalised, my father waited on me hand and foot: cooking all my meals, doing all the laundry and letting me rest. The complex weave of my self-protective armour and the pain underneath dissolved. It wasn't conscious, or worked through. It just went.

In *Invisible Cities* Marco Polo described the cities he had seen and imagined to the Chinese ruler Kublai Khan:

In Ersilia, to establish the relationships that sustain the city's life, the inhabitants stretch strings from the corners of the houses, white or black or grey or black-and-white according to whether they mark a relationship of blood, of trade, authority, agency. When the strings become so numerous that you can no longer pass among them, the inhabitants leave: the houses are dismantled; only the strings and their supports remain ...

They rebuild Ersilia elsewhere. They weave a similar pattern of strings which they would like to be more complex and at the same time more regular than the other. Then they abandon it and take themselves and their houses still farther away.

Thus, when travelling in the territory of Ersilia, you come upon the ruins of the abandoned cities without the walls which do not last, without the bones of the dead which the wind rolls away: spider-webs of intricate relationships seeking a form.

I recalled this image when I tried to conjure the words to describe what kept me standing and hoping. In the moments when I basked in the simple happiness of caring for my family and remaining healthy, the external ambitions of becoming a writer or a professional in another arena dissolved, and I just wanted to live with my friends and family around me: geographically and emotionally. What I did for a crust and the house that I lived in were not important. The strings that grounded and connected me to others were. The dress made by a relative who gave it to me and then took the time to share a cup of tea: a pink string of familial love. My son holding on like a koala and squealing with joy after I'd picked him up: a red string of blood love. My partner making me laugh: a blue string of contentment and attraction. The thought that I could call people who understood me: yellow strings of joyfulness. The knowledge that I could get on a plane and someone on the other side of the planet would welcome me into their home with real love and affection: an orange string of kindness and shared moments.

When my world fell apart on diagnosis, the criss-cross of multi-coloured connections and friendships became the flexible scaffolding that held me upright.

Every female organ apart from my brain: what makes a woman?

Choosing a doctor is difficult because it is our first explicit confrontation of our illness. 'How good is this man?' is simply the reverse of 'How bad am I?' To be sick brings out all our prejudices and primitive feelings. Like fear or love, it makes us a little crazy. Yet the craziness of the patient is part of his condition.

Anatole Broyard, 'The Patient Examines the Doctor'

Your son has a cold? asked a nurse.

Yes.

We'll have to put you in a room as people are neutropenic here.

Damn, gynaecology–oncology! Because I was having optional surgery I didn't think of the cancer side of things. A woman with no effective white blood cells could catch Celso's cold and miss out on timely surgery. I tucked his echidna puppet into his arms and hurried us past the women's magazines and health pamphlets to an open door that the head nurse gestured towards.

We bundled into a plain box that was the consulting room, and I sat down in *entertain Celso* mode. I blew up a surgical glove and let it fly around the room.

Sorry, do you mind if I change my son's nappy? He's pretty whiffy, I said to the tall man who'd appeared in front of me.

The gyn-oncology fellow cheerily replied, Of course, change his nappy. He'd just introduced himself.

I grabbed Celso's backpack and put my giggling son down on the gynaecological examination table in the adjoining room. I giggled back because the leg paddles were against my knees when normally I'd be knees up. Celso found the strange moving table and lights fascinating.

After I treble-bagged the poo we were back discussing my impending hysterectomy.

Your ovaries, fallopian tubes, uterus then cervix are taken out through your vagina.

Hmm … lovely. From what I've heard you have to blow my belly up. What's the pain through the shoulders like?

It depends on how much is used and individual reaction to pain. You'll be in hospital, so the pain will be managed.

Good. That was all I needed to know.

I found out later that the young surgeon with his Germanic clear skin, blue eyes and pretty appearance was a father of a one-year-old. Did he think of his partner's future fertility when he saw others' child-bearing years taken away, by him?

His ease with my hectic toing and froing and Celso's rambunctious destruction of the medical room wasn't so surprising in lieu of his parental knowledge.

Your last pap smear was a year and a half ago. We'll need to have another check before surgery.

Okay. *But my crotch is hairy like a bear fresh out of hibernation,* I thought.

Its aesthetic lines weren't on show under the fluorescent lights – it was just about whether there were any pre-malignant cells cooking there too and whether all my female organs could pass through my vagina.

Midway through the surgeon's scraping the sides of my vaginal wall, Celso came in grinning with a *What's going on?* look.

Oops, your son's come in, said the nurse standing to my right. A nurse was always present when male doctors did gynaecological examinations.

It doesn't matter, I replied. It's my vagina. You didn't come out of it but you grew up near it, I said to Celso.

The surgeon grinned. That's right, he said, half turning to face Celso.

Celso took a cursory look over the surgeon's shoulder. Not interested. Instead he spun the wheels on the examination table near the nurse's faux-leather pumps.

I left after three-and-a-half hours of consultations and waiting, having had:

A blood test.

A consultation and pap smear with the gyn-oncology surgeon.

Discussions in detail with a nurse who had measured my depression/anxiety levels (okay).

Discussions with my anaesthetist about my aversion to general anaesthetic. She would get my records.

A chat with a case manager: You can have a light breakfast of toast and tea then no food after 7 a.m.

And lastly a conversation with a physiotherapist, who told me what to pull and what not to. However, her first words to me on walking into the room were, Is your child disabled?

No, he's likely autistic. I smiled. *Fuck you very much*, I thought.

Afterwards in the harsh light of the room I softened my response to her, realising she'd come in armed with the information that Celso had a cold and was fed via a MIC-KEY button inserted into his stomach. His tube was stuck out of his feeding backpack. Autistics often have 'funny' guts and fussy food habits. It's not unheard of for some to require nasogastric tubes to put weight on their bones if food refusal goes on for too long. However, Celso was different from this. His was apparently a mechanical or neurological fault in his body's make-up, rather than simply a factor of autism.

I walked home wheeling Celso in the pram, well armed with what was about to happen. The public system was good. This was the first time I would have surgery for breast cancer treatment as a private patient in a public hospital.

Line up your probe at a 45-degree angle to the incision site. See? Your view is clearer.

Oh, yeah. I heard in reply through the swinging grey surgical doors, the vintage of *M*A*S*H*.

Of course this wasn't what the gyn-oncology consulting surgeon said but this was what my mind translated from his discombobulating words. He was the senior surgeon; the German gyn-oncology fellow who'd conducted my pap smear worked with him.

Hi, I'll be in in just a minute, my anaesthetist said from around the *M*A*S*H* doors. She had the sharp-eyed stare of a bird of prey. Tall and bone thin. Her intelligence radiated through her face. I liked her.

I found out later she was a mother of twins and an 18-month-old, with a nanny at home to assist.

So you're pretty fit? asked the anaesthetist's understudy. He went on, I'm studying so much I don't want to think of how unfit I am.

Buddy, I don't care if you're just a Hawking brain wheeled in here to bark orders – you being smart is good. You're brain fit then! I said.

Yes. There is that.

We started waxing lyrical about drugs. Zofran was amazing. It ceased my nausea straight away, I said.

I know, from just a wafer on the tongue. It's an excellent anti-emetic. So, what we're going to do is this … The young anaesthetist in training proceeded to explain all the drug combinations he was about to give me, which approximated five types, to stabilise me and hopefully let me wake up nausea free.

The gyn-oncology consultant bounced into the fishbowl-sized cubicle. I just want to read my notes first.

He'd accepted me on his public list after seeing me in his private suites. A kindness he could've rejected, considering I'd baulked at his surgical charges to go private.

Here he is! I said as his German colleague arrived through the swing doors. It was standing room only. From my lying-down position on the trolley his head seemed to scrape the grey ceiling.

Both men flicked pages back and forth until the consultant's notes were found.

Ah yes, I remember you now. The writer! (*If only.*) I finished my novel. I've given it to some other doctors here to read. It's 50,000 words and fairly fast paced.

Well, I handed in the first half of my MA manuscript yesterday, I said.

That must've been a good feeling.

It was! I said, thinking, *Bastard.* What I actually thought was: *Bloody hell. You, doctor, have finished an adult thriller that's on wads of paper being read by other high achievers in this hospital monolith, while – you know – consulting in public hospitals on how to save lives and running your own private surgical practice. Such a 'let's do lunch' kind of guy. I mean really.*

In truth it wasn't until this final moment with my womb and ovaries intact inside me that I actually understood what I'd agreed to, with my heart and not my head. On the trolley so close to the scalpels and metal dishes I placed my hands over my lower abdomen by way of a silent goodbye.

She has tachycardia, said someone in white.

There's a baby! My heartbeat was running too fast.

Wow! You really don't know where you are, replied my bird-of-prey anaesthetist.

No, I know I've woken from surgery but I heard a baby.

Oh yes, that's from a C-section.

Oh!

Why do they put the happy, happy post-C-section new parents with women out of gyn-oncology surgery? I'd just had my womb removed at 37 and the woman next to me just had issue from hers. What if I was childless and woke up to this?

In recovery I attached myself to a rapid-fire conversation with an African nurse, and told her how brilliant the consulting surgeon was. I held her gloved hand tight. My eyelids were heavy. I could barely see her. At intervals I peered over at the woman opposite me, who remained unconscious. Her blood pressure was dropping: 60/40. A flurry of blue-backed and white-backed nurses did something, and the unconscious woman regained consciousness briefly then was out again. Her cheekbones were angular but well padded. A relieving nurse sat slumped next to her, keeping an eye on her blood pressure. The woman looked seriously unwell. I wanted her to open her eyes.

A strutting father walked past the end of my gurney. He was followed by a new C-section mum holding their tiny baby against her chest. She appeared oblivious to the porters pushing her bed. The baby's head of hair was a swirl of red and black.

The father had walked in and out of recovery to tell relatives about the baby. His repeated knocking to be allowed back in had annoyed the staff. He had a mouth full of methadone teeth: half-rotted stumps wrought by a major addiction and its recovery. What looked like scars on his neck were scrawled tattoos. His fingers were ringed with cheap silver. He was happy. His healthy child was born. A pure moment for him and his girlfriend.

New life and the end of my capacity to nurture it.

Now: what's current in the breast cancer arena?

Quicksand years that whirl me I know not whither,
Your schemes, politics, fail — lines give way — substances
  mock and elude me;
Only the theme I sing, the great and strong-possess'd soul,
  eludes not;
One's-self must never give way — that is the final
  substance — that out of all is sure;
Out of politics, triumphs, battles, life — what at last finally
  remains?
When shows break up, what but One's-Self is sure?
  Walt Whitman, 'Quicksand Years'

In 2016, seven years after my breast cancer diagnosis, I returned to the Motherland. The last time my feet had touched British soil my mother was alive, I lived in France, my relationship with B was new and delicious, and there was no baby and no cancer in my breast. It had been 13 years. The time before javelins and arrows rained down.

I stepped onto British soil motherless, but not orphaned. I was back in the country where I was born and lived my early years. All my relatives were here. So too my oldest memories. At four trying to tie my own shoelaces on the steep stairs that led up to our second storey where our two bedrooms were: my mother's and mine. My mother had purchased our attached home when buying houses as a single mother in Brighton in the United Kingdom was possible. It was one among many row houses on Baxter Street. Mum had received the down payment on our property from her boyfriend at the time, Tony. He'd generously donated one month's interest from his trust fund to Mum to secure a home for us. Tony was the son of a wealthy Sephardic Jewish family who'd made their fortune in the cotton industry. I still have all the hats from around the world that he gave me (a collapsible top hat to go under church pews, an original pith helmet from South Africa, a public schoolboy's woollen striped hat for cricket …). Early in their relationship he'd taken her to New York to meet some of his friends. She told me that she'd been so blanketed by her own insecurities as the working-class girl from Eastbourne, and by her sense of inadequacy among his connected friends, that she'd failed to enjoy herself or be herself.

A sense of connection was always present with England. It took until I was 22 to feel Australian. Up until that point I felt English-Australian. Then I'd return to England to visit family and feel Australian-English. Never quite two feet on the soil where I was standing. Identifying as Australian took a while, but it was a relief when it finally arrived.

I'd reconnected with my grandmother by reaching out through email. She'd responded and we renewed a dead relationship. Like many adoptee stories my mother's relationship with her birth mother wasn't simple: a cellular fear of further rejection, of not being 'enough', the complexities of intense familial connection without the lived years to back it up. The fallout from their rupture in communication was that I too was disconnected from my grandmother. The second wounding for my mother of a failed relationship with her birth mother was laid to rest, before her own body was, in an exchange of letters and forgiveness the year my mother was dying.

My mother's mother stood in the entranceway of her 18th-century cottage, her pure white hair stark against the stone wall. It was a Welsh day: damp, sky dark with rain, with a strange muted green light, like reeds under water.

My grandmother stepped into her home, with its antique furniture and raging fire. It was a visitation from another world. I burst into tears. Sorry, it's just I hadn't thought about how much you looked like her, I said. It was another sliding-doors moment. This is the face my mother could have had. If she'd lived.

My grandmother didn't raise my mother but she'd developed the same purse of the lips, a similar expression in the eyes.

I'll make a cup of tea, my grandmother said. I've got cake. Chocolate, like you like.

I was so grateful. At the end of a world journey I'd returned to a place of familiarity – my mother's half-biology.

I was speaking with the woman who was my origin story. She met my mother 25 years before I did. I wanted to sit across from her and talk for weeks. I hadn't seen my grandmother in 18 years.

My grandmother's six brothers died not knowing their niece – her lost daughter – had found her. Only four of them knew their sister had a girl adopted out. A secret hidden, but heavy: passed around the dinner table in *keep quiet* glances between the brothers who held the secret to keep it from the ones who didn't. These strangers tied by blood to me knew the shadow of my mother's existence but not her substance.

I've put Heather and you in the timeline now, my grandmother said.

I hadn't travelled half a world to hear these words but they mattered all the same. My grandmother had researched and recorded her Welsh genealogy. In the table-sized printout of her work my mother and I were initially left out of the family tree. According to the records, we didn't exist.

I'd travelled to Wales because I wanted to sit across from my remaining matriarch before she died. At 89, she was sharp. During our three days of conversation at one point I couldn't find the word for the musical instrument my brother from another mother, Alexei, had played the day before in his family's Devon home. You mean pianola? she'd said without pause.

The question I wanted an answer to most was, Who was my grandfather?

I didn't get the answer of his surname, but I got others. Jim went to complete his leaving certificate with the RAF in Brighton during World War II, which is where he met my grandmother, who was doing a secretarial course. Together they created my line, but all trails of him have grown cold.

At one point, I walked up the winding, single-width stairs onto the landing outside my grandmother's own bathroom and bedroom with its view of slate, sleet and silence. Her six brothers' photographs lined the whitewashed walls. All of them were in their uniforms, young and handsome: RAF captain, second lieutenant in the army, wireless officer on tankers to a Merchant Marine. They were all dead. The last brother to die had been alive a year prior. He'd published his swansong about his journalist work as a travel writer, *The Road to Fleet Street*, just before he died. My grandmother was the last one standing of her once large family.

I am forever grateful to that police doctor. My grandmother looked down into her cup of tea.

I too looked down into my teacup, thinking about what face had been reflected back at my grandmother. I imagined a pot-bellied straight talker. Gruff in manner, but with a kind heart. A police doctor doing what he thought best for this young woman across from him. He would have served in the war only three years prior.

You're a fit, healthy young woman and you shouldn't think about an abortion, he'd said. Go ahead and have the baby, but take more care with your love life in future.

My grandmother and I also talked about her brother, who was in the Metropolitan Police Force himself, arranging for her to consult this doctor about obtaining an abortion in the early stages of the pregnancy. I owe my life to his words and my grandmother's decision. In 1948 abortion in the United Kingdom was illegal unless, according to the Preservation of Infant Life Bill, it was detrimental to the mother's health.

Returning to the UK was another victory lap, similar to the New Zealand trip that B, Celso and I took after my chemotherapy finished. This time my head of hair was back and I'd survived the crucial five years post-diagnosis cancer free. Chemicals maintained my body. The current wisdom on the oestrogen suppressor Arimidex was women should take it for ten years. I had three years to go with it in my veins every day, leaching my fat of oestrogen.

At the ten-year mark you're not cured but you join the rest of the population's chances of developing the disease – approximately one in nine for women in 'developed' countries like those in North America and western Europe. The rate in Australia is actually one in eight.

As the age of people in developed countries increases, so too does the risk of getting cancer, due to the normal process of the body's genetic integrity failing. But there's more behind the higher incidence: women from low-risk countries emigrating to high-risk countries develop similar cancer rates.

Those first standard questions Dr Wilkinson posed on meeting me – Do you smoke? How much do you drink? What's your diet like? et cetera – always gave me pause.

I clearly wasn't obese, but it would have been a red flag if I'd walked into his room fat. I did play with my reproductive life, though, by taking those white pills to keep my breast milk in, and taking the contraceptive pill for years before going off it. The answer to whether the enormous oestrogen and progesterone surges during pregnancy had combined to wake up my dormant biology and genetic predisposition to develop breast cancer remained unknowable.

For women, breast cancer is the most commonly diagnosed cancer worldwide – 25 per cent. Close to two million new cases are diagnosed per year and this appears to be rising. So too are survival rates. When I hear of this I remember that survival is often judged in terms of five years and sometimes ten. Most women diagnosed in Western countries, like Australia, have over an 80 per cent chance of surviving it – for five years. In Australia, it's the fourth-most common cause of death for women.

Breast cancer is also the most common cancer affecting Aboriginal and Torres Strait Islander women. Even though their incidence of it is lower than that of non-Indigenous women, so too are their rates of survival. This could be due to later detection and poorer outcomes in rural settings – alongside poorer advocacy for Indigenous health in general.

I was told I had an unknown genetic link with my mother due to our young age at diagnosis. Breast cancer campaigns from government supported free breast screening for 50-to-74-year-olds, and non-government fundraisers have successfully brought the high incidence of breast cancer to the public's attention – the pink ribbon is a successful marketing image, and has come to stand for breast cancer.

So too have famous actors or comedians receiving the diagnosis. After Angelina Jolie's piece appeared in *The New York Times* about her decision to remove her breasts, there was an increase among women with BRCA genes doing the same. My antennae tuned in to the debate about women having prophylactic mastectomies, but what interested me more were those who had cancer, not those who feared its likely occurrence. However, I applauded Angelina Jolie bringing the BRCA genes' existence to the public's attention.

Jennifer Saunders had triple-positive breast cancer, like me. However, she chose to keep her breast after a lumpectomy. She too sank into a depression caused by her sudden loss of a sense of youth, and taking the (anti) hormonal pill Tamoxifen. She combated her slide into the underworld with 'a little pill' that 'opened the curtains again'. When the chemo and radiotherapy finished, her hair returned, all over. She took a magnifying glass and pair of tweezers to herself.

Olivia Newton-John went a step further than writing about her experience. She lent her fame as a singer and actor and her cancer story to a flagship public hospital in Melbourne. The Olivia Newton-John Cancer Wellness and Research Centre focusses on the integration of first-rate medical science with the design of person-centred care – for example, having medical labs metres away from wards so that there is a true bench-to-bedside focus in delivering medical care. Alternative treatments such as herbal remedies and meditation are part of the program also.

Twenty-five years after Newton-John's first cancer diagnosis, it metastasised to her sacrum. You are never cured in cancer, or safe from recurrence. The sword of Damocles is with every cancer patient: every *survivor*.

What's not often discussed in the media is that breast cancer is not one-size-fits-many. There are different kinds. It can stay dormant in the duct and lobule without breaking out into surrounding tissue, meaning you're fairly safe to leave it there. This is termed DCIS and LCIS: ductal carcinoma in situ and lobular carcinoma in situ. Or it punches through the walls of the ducts and lobules to invade surrounding tissue, like what happened to my mother and me.

Paget's disease of the nipple is a rare breast cancer that forms in the nipple and areola. It's associated with invasive cancer somewhere else in the breast, and often confused with eczema due to its scaly brick-red appearance. Another invasive kind of breast cancer affects the lymphatic vessels, leaving the breast red and inflamed.

These are types of breast cancer, but that doesn't speak to their genetic make-up. In this arena there are multiple combinations. For those with a BRCA gene mutation their hormones may not play the major role in developing the disease. For my mother and me our cancers fed on oestrogen (ER+) and progesterone (PR+) to grow, with mine having the extra HER2 protein. One in five cases of breast cancer is HER2 positive. It's considered more aggressive. But you can have different levels of cancer sensitivity to your hormones. Some cancers, like mine, are highly positive to oestrogen and progesterone. Others are not. You can also develop triple-negative breast cancer (negative to hormones and the HER2 protein).

If you have a BRCA1 or 2 mutation, you have a higher chance of developing breast and ovarian cancer than the normal population. Around five to ten per cent of breast cancers have a BRCA mutation. We all have BRCA genes, but those (mainly) women who develop breast cancer from their BRCA1 mutation are more likely to test as triple negative. Those with BRCA2 mutations are more likely to have ER+ breast cancer.

But when did breast cancer first develop in the world?

From ancient times our breasts have had the ability to develop the disease. Egyptians wrote on their papyri of bulging tumours with no cure. The father of Western medicine, Hippocrates, in 460 BC described cancer as black bile, one of the body's four humours: blood, phlegm, yellow and black bile. Dutch physician Franciscus Sylvius challenged that theory in the 17th century. He said the problem was a chemical process that transformed lymphatic fluids to acidic base. Bernardino Ramazzini, the father of occupational medicine, hypothesised that a high frequency of the disease among nuns was due to a lack of sex. No sexual activity for reproductive organs meant they could decay and develop cancers. On the contrary, researcher Friedrich Hoffmann of Prussia believed sexually active women who developed the disease were having sex too vigorously, leading to lymphatic blockage. Many theories abounded from here on in about the source of women's breast disease: mental disorders, curdled milk, childlessness and a sedentary lifestyle.

The famous 17th-century painting by Rembrandt of his long-time love Hendrickje Stoffels enacting Bathsheba, King David's wife, naked at her bath, was an icon of breast cancer publicity in the 1980s. The blue-tinged dimpling on her left breast was regarded as an early visual record of the disease. Dutch scientists from the University of Twente, working on the properties of human tissue, simulated the firing of millions of photons at a tumour. They concluded it was highly unlikely the painting was a depiction of breast cancer based on discolouration, and that the eye would only pick up a blue tinge caused by breast tumours if they were located one to three millimetres under the skin. As most tumours are much deeper than this, it diminished Bathsheba's usefulness as an iconic image. Though dimpling in a breast can mean cancer's present.

The 18th-century French physician Henri Le Dran said that removal of the tumour and infected lymph nodes in the armpit helped treat breast cancer. A pioneer in cataract surgery and the removal of bladder stones, Claude-Nicolas Le Cat argued surgical removal was the only treatment. These beliefs led to the creation of the radical mastectomy as the best medical response to breast cancer.

By the 19th and 20th centuries, with the development of better medical care, like antiseptics, anaesthesia and blood transfusions, people survived surgery in far greater numbers. William Halsted introduced the en bloc radical mastectomy into surgical practice. His method was to remove the breast, axillary nodes in the armpit, and the chest muscle. This became the go-to response to breast cancer for 100 years. The radical mastectomy remained common practice four decades into the 20th century.

The development of a systemic theory took over when ovaries and then adrenal glands were removed by surgeons once the discovery that reducing oestrogen in the bloodstream reduced tumour size.

In 1976 Bernard Fisher began a study that would show that breast cancer patients had the same survival rate whether they underwent a radical mastectomy or less invasive surgery followed by radiation and chemotherapy. Dr Fisher, a former specialist in liver regeneration and transplantation, joined I.S. Ravdin's National Surgical Adjuvant Breast and Bowel Project. Dr Fisher's decades of clinical trials and laboratory research into tumour metastasis led to a surgical shift away from Halsted's radical mastectomy.

Modern medicine has seen huge leaps in novel therapies for breast cancer, like hormone treatments, and better surgical and biological therapies. Mammograms and ultrasounds have been developed for early detection. Genes have been isolated that cause breast cancer: BRCA1, BRCA2 and ATM. The ATM (ataxia-telangiectasia mutated) gene helps control the rate at which cells divide and grow. Scientists are finding or have found many other gene mutations, as in the HER2-amplified breast cancer I had, that play a role in causing tumours to grow.

The new way in breast cancer and its treatment is in the arena of personalised medicine and gene therapy. I can imagine a day when 'good cells' are used, by extracting, medically tweaking and then returning them to the body, to attack and kill cancer cells instead of chemotherapy. When this happens cancer patients can live a life while going through treatment without extreme ill health and hair loss. My fingers are crossed, big time, for this to become standard treatment in my lifetime.

I live with cancer every day. I choose to do this, as a reminder that my future death wants me to live well now. The bodily truth of its one-time existence is writ large: I see it in the shower and in the mirror – my portacath peekaboo scar atop my left breast. When the breast surgeon removed nine lymph nodes from my armpit, one of them a nugget of cancer, I developed cording. It's like a thin rope pulled taut under my flesh, my skin forming a tent along its raised seam, from the breast, to the armpit and down the arm. I have this tugging at my flesh every day.

Seven years of taking Arimidex atrophied my vagina. With such low levels of oestrogen floating around I shot into my 60s, it seemed. Now I looked at women over 60, in their 70s, and officially old in their 80s, and saw the unspoken. The first national study, *Sex, Age & Me: A National Study of Sex and Relationships Among Australians Aged 60+*, showed a mild movement in the media about acknowledging ageism around 'old age' people having a sexual life. I was 42, but felt a projected kinship. I never heard mention of penetrative intercourse being a part of that life. Did most women, years into menopause, have vaginal walls so thin that penetration could hurt like a razor blade?

The Women's Wellness Research Program, run out of Griffith University and affiliated with the Queensland University of Technology, has developed a 12-step intervention called the Women's Wellness After Cancer Program, which addresses some of these issues. The program has shown significant results for women's sense of happiness, measured in terms of reducing weight and improved sexual self-efficacy. I did casual work for this program as a research assistant on the dataset results.

In moments of contentment I'm the original Amazonian who cut off her right breast to shoot straighter. I did everything to live for myself and for my son. Bereaved spouses find other partners after the death of their significant others. B would find another mate – my son would no longer have his mother if I died early.

With the return of a new normal, some of the rapidly made decisions leading into my first lot of surgeries came back to haunt me a little. I attended the 43rd Clinical Oncology Society of Australia's joint conference with the Breast Cancer Trials group to take part in advocacy training around improving clinical-trial participation in Australia. The current knowledge and work in the breast cancer space is on neoadjuvant therapy, meaning if you get a breast cancer diagnosis now you can go straight into more refined chemotherapy regimens and, depending on your tumour type, you may not require such invasive surgery. You might preserve your breasts with the same survival rates as mastectomy. Of course this depends on your particular brand of cancer.

My double mastectomy I have no qualms about, nor my chemotherapy regimen, administered under a clinical trial where I took a particularly toxic form of drug, one of the taxanes, which can leave you permanently bald and with reduced heart function. One choice stirred regrets when I reached 42. I had been asked if I wanted to preserve my eggs before undergoing chemotherapy. I refused. When my period returned soon after finishing chemotherapy I was told I needed to shut my ovaries down due to them pumping out the very hormone that triggered my cancer. I chose to remove my womb, ovaries, fallopian tubes and cervix. Would it have been possible to have another child post–cancer treatment if I'd left myself intact?

I'll never know.

I'd wanted more children. The grief around this came back – not in full blaring horns of *Shit, what did I do?*, but in a slow, dripping way – in *That wasn't what I'd wanted* pangs. The kind of sadness like a shadow that sometimes you notice and are at other times entirely unaware of. I'm sorry, future second child, we'll never meet.

The truth of my birthing Celso – my first near-death experience – and my developing an aggressive form of breast cancer within my son's first year of life is that my body was not well suited to making babies. I wish it were different, but it's not. The combination of a likely genetic tweak behind my son's 'abilities' and my kind of cancer meant bearing children was dangerous for me.

In Australia, I cannot adopt a child because I've had breast cancer and now likely because of my age – 42. Of course, birth mothers get cancer but government human services have decreed that placing a child with an adoptive mother who might die prematurely is too great a risk of another grief. Clearly, the wisdom of this doesn't follow national statistics on survival rates or look to the father's ability to be an excellent parent – solo or not. All that aside, my mother's experience of adoption made me pause. Would I be doing the child a favour? Is it really about them or about me wanting a 'normal' child? Is it because I want a playmate for Celso to develop his social skills, and not about openheartedly loving another child? Truthfully, I'd hope for all of these: the joy of witnessing a daughter or son develop normally, and the benefits this could reap for Celso.

This year, ten years after my mother's death, I received a strange phone call.

Is this Josepha Ruth Dietrich?

Yes, I said, getting ready to end the sales conversation.

This may seem strange, but we've done an audit on all our superannuation accounts and we didn't pay all of your late mother's estate.

I looked up at the ceiling with its bare light-bulb and thanked my mother – again. I was two weeks out from finishing a contract as a research assistant with the psychiatry department of the University of Queensland's Faculty of Medicine. The quality improvement project I was working on trained psychiatric nurses in motivational interviewing to improve the discharge planning process for people coming out of inpatient psychiatric units. I'd first returned as a casual then taken this part-time position when Celso was five years old. Now, just as it wrapped up, came a much-needed windfall from my mum.

In 2017, at nine years old, all of Celso's front teeth are loose. He has one cartoon gap – an empty square against his other teeth – when he smiles. The tooth fairy hasn't visited his pillow with money as yet. This is so Celso:

Stalled

stalled

then ...

change.

He's taught me so much about not hanging onto expectations.

He attends a mainstream school with an integration aide in the classroom with him, helping to interpret class work and engage with his peers and wonderful teachers. Our local school community opened their arms to Celso. Certain children gravitate towards him in the playground, making him their special friend; these are usually those with some emotional experience too hard for their young selves to understand yet, like arriving in Australia without English and having to acquire the language quickly, or those classed as different in some way, who find Celso's non-judgemental acceptance of them a relief.

I've organised outside professionals – an occupational therapist with years of experience with atypical children, and a music therapist who's focussing on his speech – to attend the school for therapy sessions each week. The primary school's enrichment education co-ordinator has put together a team of the best aides, young and vibrant, the school speech therapist and the pick of the teachers who *get* my son. Until year three he only attended four days a week. In agreement with the school, Celso required time away and Fridays were Son-Rise Program days, where play therapists worked on social engagement, eye contact and vocalising. Even now Celso finishes school at 2 p.m., finding his energy permits this and not more.

Post–cancer treatments, I signed up to ride more than 200 kilometres over two days to raise money for breast cancer research by the QIMR Berghofer Medical Research Institute. Over five years my Breast Friends for a Cure team raised just over $120,000 and cycled hundreds of kilometres in training and during event weekends. This led to my meeting the CEO of QIMR and some of their fabulous scientists. Through these connections I got a position going out into the community and into businesses to speak about the Ride events. The job was part sales, part inspirational talker, part fundraiser. CauseForce, who ran the events, raised millions for cancer research.

The sales component of the job fitted like a man's suit and, after my second trip to the Autism Treatment Center of America to train in the Son-Rise process that helped my son, I walked into the office, and sat down. By day's end I'd resigned. For a year I'd put my hat in the ring of doing something to raise large sums of money for cancer research. Stepping out under the ropes, I found a position that so much better reflected my psychology background and more of my values in the research assistant position that was just coming to an end when Mum's extra super turned up.

Another surprise outcome of my participating in the Ride events was getting selected, alongside another of my Breast Friends for a Cure teammates, to be featured in a coffee table book: *Under the Red Dress*. Beth Whaanga and her friend, photographer Nadia Masot, created this project after Beth posted photographs of herself on Facebook after mastectomy and reconstruction. A hundred 'friends' de-friended her and this led to a campaign, in photographer Nadia's words: *to build awareness around cancer and cancer-related stigma, particularly regarding the grievous bodily scarring that results from surgery and treatment. To destigmatise issues around disease taboos in society ... to play a part in redefining the world's idea of 'beauty' and unattainable perfection.*

I also became an active cancer patient advocate with CanSpeak Queensland, the voice of the cancer community, which led to a position on the Community Board Advisory Group (CBAG) for the Metro North Hospital and Health Service – the largest one in Australia. CBAG provides advice to the Metro North Hospital Board on consumer and community engagement to improve health outcomes for communities in Metro North Brisbane.

My mother's campaigns for equal rights for women and an adoptee's legal right to know their mother's information stood behind me as a reminder that 'turning up' to contribute in public life makes a difference. My survival was one legacy of my mother's premature death; another was my own mission to try and reduce the chances of other mothers dying young.

Celso's diagnosis and hope

But if I'm not the same, the next question is, 'Who in the world am I?' Ah, that's the great puzzle!

Alice talking to The Rabbit

Lewis Carroll, *Alice's Adventures in Wonderland*

I have no qualms diagnosing your son as having autistic behaviours, so now you can apply for government funding, said the developmental paediatrician. He was South African, wore a pink-striped shirt and aligned his desk's writing pad so it sat square to the tabletop.

Great! I said and meant it. Celso's exclusive activities, like reading book after book about birds while avoiding all eye contact, were clues that he tended towards an Autism Spectrum Disorder.

A label was helpful to tell others, but mostly useful for B and me. When strangers asked with raised eyebrows and upwards inflections, And how old is your son?

He's three, I'd say, then feel a need to explain him.

When we first started Celso on the Son-Rise Program around his fourth birthday, it felt like convincing a child from

Atlantis to break the watery surface between us and enter my world. We set his bedroom up with high shelves, mirrors and padded floor, so I could run the play-based therapy in his bedroom. The high shelves were for getting distractions, like toys, off the floor and up high, and if he wanted something he needed to communicate with someone to get it (this sounds punitive, but it wasn't). This basic-sounding idea for communication was very effective. Celso's eye contact improved remarkably as he was so keen to get his Schleich toys or his books.

The mirrors were for communication too. It was less demanding on Celso to look at you via the mirror – like being at one remove from direct eye contact, something most people with autism feel acutely. The padded floor was for comfort in play.

Celso was squirming his way to the middle of a springy child's tunnel. I grabbed the reinforced circles and picked up the tunnel and him, held him up in the air, then lowered him gently down. His end-of-the-broomstick sharp little feet punched out through the fabric.

I'm hungry! Yum, yum, yum. I pretended to bite his feet.

He was squealing, excited, a bit frightened – happy.

I pulled down the lip of one end of the tunnel and Celso stared with his pearl teeth exposed with bright-eyed laughter into my face.

I love it when you look at me! I pointed to my eyes.

He was maintaining eye contact. *Should I milk the moment with positive reinforcement?* Instead, I smiled back at him and continued bite-play.

Since we'd started therapy he had gone off all medication and started eating, drinking water, spelling up to 50 words like *echidna* with his wooden blocks, or typing them out on our computer. His eye contact had improved considerably, he sought us out for cuddles and kisses, he gestured and expressed wants and needs. And most noticeably his receptive language had turned on. He understood and responded to everything we said. We were on our way. I didn't know how far Celso would swim up to the surface of our world from his Atlantis, but he was swimming – I could make out the clear lines of his face now.

As the year drew to a close I received my Master of Arts (Research). I had written that novel in the end, a young adult fantasy. It wasn't published, but it existed out of my mind and on the page.

I'd spent my 30s wrestling myself back from the jump into the unrecoverable: grief, madness, death. I held the image of myself like a hand mirror. Up until my mother's death I'd have said, You're the stable one. I didn't know if that was so true anymore. Mainly I glimpsed the bright, real rays of hope in a life – the life I was given. The exquisite working mind and working heart of a healthy body. Every day I had a daily *Oh gods thank you* when I caught myself throwing Celso into the air with the strength of my non-cancerous body. Fingers crossed, may it last as long as humanly possible.

The word *heaven* kept popping into my mind. I said this often. I had no desire to reach the Christian version, but rather the children's author Philip Pullman's idea of a republic of heaven on earth. It wasn't always pretty and kind but four years on from breast cancer I'd reached my own republic.

My life had been saved three times. The first by a surgeon's hands after the birth of my son. The second was by my mother's death and its education of the better medical choices to make on my diagnosis. The third: by writing. I needed it to access a language of grief, buried ambition and hopes for a future I wanted, but didn't know how to reach. Writing my life was the second helix coil twisting and turning inside me rebuilding my body.

My mother and I in November 2005,
one month before her death

Acknowledgements

To my partner, B, and our son, Celso, thank you. To the family and friends that flocked around us during the time when arrows and javelins rained down – thank you.

For my mentor on the final run-through of the manuscript – the real work – Kristina Olsson, you are a wise writer and a joy to be around, thank you. To my publisher, Alexandra Payne, and editor, Ian See, from UQP – thank you for taking a punt on me, an unknown voice among many writers trying to get their work published. To Kate O'Donnell, who delicately took my manuscript into her editor's hands and made insightful, spot-on comments on what worked and what didn't as a 'first reader' – thank you.

It took knocking on the door, over many years, to finally have one night where the stars aligned – a salon reading where the right people were in the room listening: Krissy Kneen (who introduced me to my agent, Jane Novak) and Jill Eddington (newly minted CEO of UQP) – thank you.

Resources

These resources helped me during my cancer regimen, pre- and post-treatment:

- **The Wesley Hospital Choices Cancer Support Centre** matched me with a woman a bit further along the treatment regimen than I was, so I could discuss what was happening to me with someone who knew. Choices has a network of professionals that can offer expert clinical advice, specialist peer support, yoga and art classes, bra fittings (on-site) for women after mastectomy, and many other important services. All free!

- **Mater Chicks in Pink** provided funds for a nanny to care for my son when he was in hospital and I couldn't attend to him. They ran a Mindful Parenting program for women who had children and were going through breast cancer treatment. I met my Right Wingers (support group) there – three other women with right breast cancers: Briony, Katie and Linda. These women have become a lifeline for me. We share a unique bond forged through very difficult times and remain a constant support to one another, catching up regularly to check in on how we're faring.

- Ten sessions provided (FYI: this is per calendar year, folks) by Medicare to see a **psychologist**.

- A **hospital psychiatrist**, free of charge, accessed through the Royal Brisbane and Women's Hospital for the length of my chemotherapy – she saw me on ward during treatments.

- **Mummy's Wish** provided funding for a house cleaner during part of my chemotherapy, so I didn't have to clean the house while trying to care for my son.

- A **family GP**: get one who is the right fit for you, and who also knows lots of stuff and advocates for you to receive the services available in Australia.

- A **road bike** helped me to get fit again and feel my body come back to life.

- **Cancer Council Queensland** provided funding for my synthetic wig 'Tiana' (purchased through Starkles).

- **Look Good Feel Better** offers a free one-off workshop for women on dealing with the appearance-related side effects of cancer treatment (the workshop includes free make-up).

- **The Ride to Conquer Cancer**, benefitting the QIMR Berghofer Medical Research Institute: my team, Breast Friends for a Cure, focussed on raising money for breast and gynaecological cancer research as a way to give back to the science community that kept us alive. The ride also created a focus for exercising regularly. I ended up working for CauseForce, who run the Ride and Walk events, as my first job after my treatments finished and my son was in school.

- **The Weekend to End Women's Cancers**: I was volunteer captain of the caboose team of cyclists on the walk route, providing support and encouragement to the walkers who were raising money by taking part in the event. Connecting with a cancer community helped a great deal during this period of time. It gave a sense of meaning to what had just happened to me and others.

- **Denise Stewart**, whom I call a magical witch for her capacity to show me how to stretch my scars to fix cording and stiffening after my numerous surgeries, is a well-informed and proactive professional in her field of occupational therapy. I accessed her services through the Mater Private Breast Cancer Centre.

- **Breast Cancer Network Australia** provided a My Journey Kit (a free information pack), which I turned to regularly to read and check what I was being told by doctors.

- I was a control participant on the **BETH clinical trial**, which tested if the drug Bevacizumab plus Trastuzumab (Herceptin) increased survival rates for women with HER2-positive breast cancer. The research nurse checked me regularly and was a go-to person if I had questions about side effects. I felt closely monitored, which helped alleviate anxiety, and my involvement contributed to furthering the knowledge around breast cancer and its treatments.

- **Family and friends:** build a scaffolding around you of people whom you're comfortable with and love – people you can ask for help, knowing you'll receive it!

Bibliography

ABC Radio National, *In Conversation: Elizabeth Blackburn*, radio program, 15 March 2007. http://www.abc.net.au/radionational/programs/inconversation/elizabeth-blackburn/3395776

Anderson-Dargatz, Gail, *The Cure for Death by Lightning*, Vintage Canada, Toronto, 1997.

Armstrong, Lance, and Jenkins, Sally, *It's Not About the Bike: My Journey Back to Life*, Penguin, New York, 2000.

Broyard, Anatole, 'The Patient Examines the Doctor', *Intoxicated by My Illness: And Other Writings on Life and Death*, Fawcett Columbine, New York, 1992, pp. 36 and 44. Excerpts on pp. 165 and 180 copyright © 1992 by the Estate of Anatole Broyard. Used by permission of Clarkson Potter/Publishers, an imprint of the Crown Publishing Group, a division of Penguin Random House LLC. All rights reserved. Any third party use of this material, outside of this publication, is prohibited. Interested parties must apply directly to Penguin Random House LLC for permission.

Buxton, Nigel, *The Road to Fleet Street: An Autobiography*, New Barn Books, Great Britain, 2015.

Calvino, Italo, *Invisible Cities* (tr. William Weaver), Vintage Books, London, 1997, p. 68. Excerpt on pp. 178–179 copyright © 1972 by Giulio Einaudi editore, s.p.a. Torino, English translation copyright © 1983, 1984 by Houghton Mifflin Harcourt Publishing Company. Reprinted by permission of Houghton Mifflin Harcourt Publishing Company. All rights reserved. Also published by Secker & Warburg. Reproduced by permission of The Random House Group Ltd. © 1974

Cancer Australia, 'Breast Cancer Statistics', Commonwealth of Australia, Sydney, 2017. https://breast-cancer.canceraustralia.gov.au/statistics

Carroll, Lewis, *Alice's Adventures in Wonderland*, Macmillan, London, 1920, p. 19.

Cavallo, Jo, 'Dr Bernard Fisher's Breast Cancer Research Left a Lasting Legacy of Improved Therapeutic Efficacy and Survival', *The ASCO Post*, 15 May 2013. http://www.ascopost.com/issues/may-15-2013/dr-bernard-fishers-breast-cancer-research-left-a-lasting-legacy-of-improved-therapeutic-efficacy-and-survival.aspx

Dickinson, Emily, 'I Felt My Life with Both My Hands', *Emily Dickinson: Selected Poems*, Phoenix, London, 2010, p. 27.

Didion, Joan, *The Year of Magical Thinking*, Vintage Books, New York, 2006, pp. 57 and 198. Quotes on pp. 90 and 120 reprinted with permission of Penguin Random House and HarperCollins Publishers Ltd. © Joan Didion 2006

Dietrich, Heather, 'Motherhood and the Feminist Vision: The Lesson from the New Reproductive Technologies', *FINRRAGE: Feminist International Network of Resistance to Reproductive and Genetic Engineering*, vol. 2, no. 10, 1991, pp. 7–12.

Dietrich, Josepha, 'Next of Kin', *Honestly Woman: Business Magazine*, June–August 2007, pp. 38–39.

Doidge, Norman, *The Brain That Changes Itself: Stories of Personal Triumph from the Frontiers of Brain Science*, Penguin, New York, 2007.

Dr Seuss, *Oh, the Places You'll Go!*, HarperCollins, London, 2012.

Follett, Barbara (eds Harold Grier McCurdy and Helen Follett), *Barbara: The Unconscious Autobiography of a Child Genius*, University of North Carolina Press, Chapel Hill, 1966, p. 107. Quote on p. 83 copyright © 1966 by the University of North Carolina Press. Used by permission of the publisher. www.uncpress.org

Gaskell, Elizabeth, *North and South*, Wordsworth Editions, London, 1994, p. 17.

Gilbert, Elizabeth, *Eat, Pray, Love: A Memoir*, Viking, New York, 2007.

——, *The Signature of All Things*, Bloomsbury Publishing Plc, London, 2013, p. 529. Quote on p. 123 © Elizabeth Gilbert, 2013. Reproduced with kind permission of Penguin Random House US and Bloomsbury UK.

Goldgar, David E., Healey, Sue, et al., 'Rare Variants in the ATM Gene and Risk of Breast Cancer', *Breast Cancer Research*, vol. 13, no. 4, 2011.

Gornick, Vivian, *Fierce Attachments: A Memoir*, Daunt Books, New York, 1987.

——, *The Situation and The Story: The Art of Personal Narrative*, Farrar, Straus and Giroux, New York, 2002, p. 92. Copyright © 2001 by Vivian Gornick. Quote on p. 66 reprinted by permission of Farrar, Straus and Giroux.

Groopman, Jerome, *The Anatomy of Hope: How People Find Strength in the Face of Illness*, Simon & Schuster, London, 2004, p. 81. Quote on p. 153 reproduced with kind permission of the author.

Hayward, Helen, 'My Children, My Life', *aeon magazine*, 2014; also published in *A Slow Childhood: Notes on Thoughtful Parenting*, Editia, Sydney, 2017. Quote on p. 131 reproduced with kind permission of the author.

Hecht, Jennifer Michael, 'My Hero', *Who Said*, Copper Canyon Press, Port Townsend, Washington, 2013, p. 17. Quote on p. 141 copyright

© 2013 by Jennifer Michael Hecht. Reprinted with the permission of The Permissions Company, Inc. on behalf of Copper Canyon Press, www.coppercanyonpress.org.

Hitchens, Christopher, 'Miss Manners and the Big C', *Vanity Fair*, no. 604, December 2010.

Hustvedt, Siri, *The Shaking Woman, or a History of My Nerves*, Hodder and Stoughton, London, 2011, p. 116. Quote on p. 157 copyright © 2011 by Siri Hustvedt. Reproduced by John Murray Press, a division of Hodder and Stoughton Limited.

Jamie, Kathleen, 'Pathologies: A Startling Tour of Our Bodies', *Granta 102: The New Nature Writing*, Summer 2008, pp. 42–43. Quote on p. 3 reproduced with kind permission of the author.

Jolie, Angelina, 'My Medical Choice', *The New York Times*, 14 May 2013, p. A25.

Lane, Bernard, and Dayton, Leigh, 'Nobel First for Aussie Woman', *The Australian*, 6 October 2009, pp. 1–2.

LeGuin, Ursula K., *The Earthsea Quartet*, Puffin, London, 1993.

Lyons, Anthony, Heywood, Wendy, et al., *Sex, Age & Me: A National Study of Sex and Relationships Among Australians Aged 60+*, Australian Research Centre in Sex, Health and Society, La Trobe University, Melbourne, 2017. sexageme.org.au

Mandal, Ananya, 'History of Breast Cancer', *News-Medical.Net*, 22 September 2013. https://www.news-medical.net/health/History-of-Breast-Cancer.aspx

Manderson, Lenore, *Surface Tensions: Surgery, Bodily Boundaries, and the Social Self*, Left Coast Press, Walnut Creek, 2011.

Mukherjee, Siddhartha, *The Emperor of All Maladies: A Biography of Cancer*, Fourth Estate, London, 2011.

Oliver, Mary, 'In Blackwater Woods', *New and Selected Poems, Volume One*, Beacon Press, Boston, 1992, p. 177. Originally from *American*

Primitive by Mary Oliver. Copyright © 1983 by Mary Oliver. Reprinted with the permission of Little, Brown and Company. All rights reserved.

Pausch, Randy, and Zaslow, Jeffrey, *The Last Lecture*, Hyperion, New York, 2008.

Plath, Sylvia, *The Bell Jar*, HarperCollins, New York, 1971. Quote on p. 170 from pages 85–86 ('I saw my life ... at my feet.') copyright © 1971 by Harper & Row, Publishers, Inc. Reprinted by permission of HarperCollins Publishers and Faber & Faber Ltd.

Porter, Dorothy, 'Not the Same', *The Bee Hut*, Black Inc., Melbourne, 2009, p. 60. © Dorothy Porter, 2009. Reproduced with permission of Jenny Darling Associates Literary Agent.

Porter-Steele, Janine, 'Sexuality and Body Image in Women Following Diagnosis and Treatment for Cancer: Evaluation of an E-Health Enabled Intervention', Women's Wellness After Cancer Program, Queensland University of Technology, PhD project.

Pullman, Philip, *His Dark Materials: Collected Edition*, Scholastic, London, 2008.

Saunders, Jennifer, *Bonkers: My Life in Laughs*, Viking, Melbourne, 2013.

Servan-Schreiber, David, *Anticancer: A New Way of Life*, Viking, New York, 2009.

Shulman, Lawrence N., Willett, Walter, et al., 'Breast Cancer in Developing Countries: Opportunities for Improved Survival', *Journal of Oncology*, vol. 2010, Article ID 595167, 2010.

Sontag, Susan, *Illness as Metaphor and AIDS and Its Metaphors*, Penguin, New York, 1991, p. 3. Copyright © 1977, 1978 by Susan Sontag. Quote on p. 8 reproduced by permission of Farrar, Straus and Giroux, and Penguin Random House UK.

Vickers, Salley, *The Other Side of You*, Fourth Estate, London, 2006, p. 90. Quote on p. 124 reprinted by permission of Farrar, Straus and Giroux, and HarperCollins Publishers Ltd. © 2006 Salley Vickers

Walker, Brenda, *Reading by Moonlight: How Books Saved a Life*, Hamish Hamilton, Melbourne, 2010, p. 143. Quote on p. 92 reproduced with kind permission of the author.

Weston, Gabriel, *Direct Red: A Surgeon's Story*, Vintage Books, London, 2010, pp. 1, 36, 61.

Whitman, Walt, 'Quicksand Years', *Leaves of Grass: And Other Writings*, W.W. Norton & Company, Inc., New York, 2002, p. 376.

Williams, Florence, *Breasts: A Natural and Unnatural History*, W.W. Norton & Company, Inc., New York, 2012, p. 231. Quote on p. 87 reproduced with kind permission of W.W. Norton & Company, Inc.

Woolf, Virginia, *On Being Ill*, Paris Press, Ashfield, Massachusetts, 2002, pp. 3–4. Quote on p. 56 reproduced by kind permission of The Society of Authors as the Literary Representative of the Estate of Virginia Woolf.

Wyndham, Susan, *Life in His Hands: The True Story of a Neurosurgeon and a Pianist*, Picador, Sydney, 2008.